D1083328

SPORT SHOES
AND
PLAYING SURFACES

Biomechanical Properties

E.C. Frederick, PhD
Director of Research
Nike Sport Research Laboratory
Exeter, New Hampshire

Human Kinetics Publishers, Inc.
Champaign, Illinois 61820

Production Director: Kathryn Gollin Marshak
Editorial Staff: Peg Goyette, John Sauget
Typesetter: Sandra Meier
Text Layout: Denise Peters
Cover Design: Jack Davis

Library of Congress Catalog Number: 83-083166
ISBN: 0-931250-51-X

Printed in the United States of America

Human Kinetics Publishers, Inc.
Box 5076
Champaign, IL 61820

Contributing Authors

Baudzus, Wolfgang, Institut fur Biomechanik, Deutsche Sporthochschule Koln, Carl-Diem-Weg, D-5000 Koln, BRD.

Baumann, Wolfgang, Institut fur Biomechanik, Deutsche Sporthochschule Koln, Carl-Diem-Weg, D-5000 Koln, BRD.

Cavanagh, Peter R., Biomechanics Laboratory, Pennsylvania State University, University Park, Pennsylvania 16802, USA.

Clarke, Thomas E., Nike Sport Research Laboratory, 156 Front Street, Exeter, New Hampshire 03833, USA.

Cuin, David E., International Athletic Surface Consultants, Inc., 95 Madison Avenue, Morristown, New Jersey 07960, USA.

Denoth, Jachen, Biomechanics Laboratory, Swiss Federal Institute of Technology (ETH) Weinbergstrasse 98, CH-8006 Zurich, Switzerland.

Frederick, Edward C., Nike Sport Research Laboratory, 156 Front Street, Exeter, New Hampshire 03833, USA.

Greene, Peter R., BGKT, Ltd., 153 Main Street, Huntington, New York 11743, USA.

Hamill, Clare, Nike Sport Research Laboratory, 156 Front Street, Exeter, New Hampshire 03833, USA.

Kerr, Barry, Biomechanics Laboratory, Faculty of Physical Education, The University of Calgary, 2500 University Drive NW, Calgary, Alberta T2N 1N4, Canada.

Kolitzus, H.J., Institut fur Sportbodentechnik, Basadingerstrasse 40, CH-8253 Diessenhofen, Switzerland.

Luethi, Simon, Biomechanics Laboratory, Faculty of Physical Education, The University of Calgary, 2500 University Drive NW, Calgary, Alberta T2N 1N4, Canada.

MacLellan, Gordon E., 35 Branksome Way, Kenton Harrow, Middlesex HA3 95H, UK.

McMahon, Thomas A., Department of Applied Sciences, Harvard University, Pierce Hall, Cambridge, Massachusetts 02138, USA.

Misevich, Kenneth W., Colgate-Palmolive Company, Research and Development, 909 River Road, Piscataway, New Jersey 08854, USA.

Nigg, Benno M., Biomechanics Laboratory, Faculty of Physical Education, The University of Calgary, 2500 University Drive NW, Calgary, Alberta T2N 1N4, Canada.

Smith, David, Biomechanics Laboratory, Faculty of Physical Education, The University of Calgary, 2500 University Drive NW, Calgary, Alberta T2N 1N4, Canada.

Stacoff, Alex, Biomechanics Laboratory, Swiss Federal Institute of Technology (ETH) Weinbergstrasse 98, CH-8006 Zurich, Switzerland.

Stucke, Helmut, Institut fur Biomechanik, Deutsche Sporthochschule Koln, Carl-Diem-Weg, D-5000 Koln, BRD.

Valiant, Gordon A., Biomechanics Laboratory, Pennsylvania State University, University Park, Pennsylvania 16802, USA.

Contents

Preface

A book about the biomechanical properties of sport shoes and playing surfaces could not have been written 10 years ago. The current frenzied state of research interest in this area is certainly, in part, a coincidence of the current renaissance in sport biomechanics. However, it appears to be due to more than that. Much of this activity seems to stem from the excitement generated by the simple discovery that shoes and surfaces make a difference.

Athletes have always felt that shoe design and surface characteristics have an effect on performance and injury. Tracks, for example, have often been rumored to be "slow," "fast," or a "crippler," and footwear has been the object of even more ergogenic and etiologic speculation. Scientists, on the other hand, largely dismissed these observations as speculative or merely psychological. It is only in the last decade that we have been able to quantify such effects and to see that the athlete's observations hold some truth. We are now beginning to understand some of the significant biomechanical features of shoes and surfaces that may enhance performance or affect injury.

This collection of review articles discusses many of those effects. You will learn in the pages that follow that, among other effects, shoes and surfaces significantly alter the kinematics of running and jumping; have qualities that may allow athletes to run faster or jump higher or farther; and can cause or prevent injury and possibly speed recovery. In addition to these findings, this book also reviews many of the test methods used to evaluate shoes and surfaces and discusses the controversial application of the surface-related tests to the establishment of standards for sport surfaces.

This kind of information may be helpful or even essential to the coach, athlete, physician, podiatrist, therapist, physical educator, or administrator who must make informed recommendations or decisions about the use of particular sport shoes or playing surfaces. Consider, for example, the physician who has to diagnose a patient's injury. It may well be that a contributing factor in the etiology of the injury is the surface or shoe. The results of many studies on the relationship between injury and various surface or shoe characteristics are reviewed in this volume. It is a major objective of this book that this sort of information be accessible to the very people who are most likely to apply it.

Chapter 1 is by Benno Nigg and co-workers at the University of Calgary and the Swiss Federal Institute of Technology in Zurich, where Nigg was director of the biomechanics laboratory for several years. This paper is a review of the methods developed by Nigg and others for assessing the load on the human body in various sports movements. It also summarizes the results of recent research on the relationship between surface and sport shoe characteristics and the etiology of various athletic injuries. Much of the work that is cited in this paper has never before appeared in English, making this review all the more valuable.

Chapter 2, by Peter Cavanagh of Pennsylvania State University, is linked to Ken Misevich's Chapter 3. These two papers present a model of the interaction of shoe and foot during foot contact in running. Cavanagh's paper reviews the relevant literature and presents the results of new research on the physical properties of the subcalcaneal fat pad—an essential part of the body's shock-attenuating capability. Cavanagh's work raises many questions about the mechanical consequences of pathological changes in this structure, and he discusses the relevance of these findings to the design and selection of proper footwear.

Misevich, of Colgate-Palmolive's Research and Development Department, reports on the results of extensive tests of midsole and heel wedge materials, and describes a mathematical model that defines the dynamic physical properties of midsole and wedge materials as they are loaded during the collision of the foot with the ground during running. These findings are relevant in the design of prostheses as well as the development and selection of safe sport shoes.

Chapter 4, by Gordon MacLellan of the Royal National Orthopedic Hospital in London, describes his attempts to reduce the shock to the musculoskeletal system by using viscoelastic shoe inserts. MacLellan also discusses the results of clinical trials using these pads to treat patients with chronic problems that he believes are caused or exacerbated by impact shock.

Chapter 5 is by Helmut Stucke of the Biomechanics Institute of the Deutsche Sporthochschule in Cologne. The paper describes the work of Stuke and his collaborators, Wolfgang Baudzus and Wolfgang Baumann, on measuring the traction of various playing surfaces. Their work highlights the difficulty in making valid and reliable traction measurements and calls into question the results of other investigators. Traction is a critical characteristic of safe, performance sport surfaces; and their work is a key contribution to the development of accurate measurements that can be used in the design and selection of proper surface materials.

Chapter 6 is by H.J. Kolitzus, the controversial author of many of the DIN standards for playing surfaces throughout West Germany. This paper discusses his approach to standardization and describes his test methods in detail.

Chapters 7 and 8 contain papers previously published in the *Journal of Biomechanics* by the Harvard team of Tom McMahon and Peter Greene. Their work suggests that optimal surfaces for running should have surface elastic properties that fall within a range of values defined by empirical data and a model they present describing the spring stiffness of the human body while running on surfaces of variable stiffness. This is one of the most exciting new ideas in current biomechanics and their findings have been used to construct several "tuned" tracks on which many national and world records have been set.

To highlight this, David Cuin, a representative of En-Tout-Cas, Ltd., briefly describes in Chapter 9 the design and construction of a high performance track that applies the principles set forth by McMahon and Greene.

Chapters 10 and 11 are by the team of Tom Clarke, Ned Frederick, and Clare Hamill of the Nike Sport Research Laboratory. Their papers review the methodology used to make rearfoot kinematic and cushioning measurements and then to apply the results of these measurements to a group of 36 specially constructed shoes. The design variables analyzed in these studies are midsole hardness, shoe thickness, and the angle of flare at the rear part of the shoe. These data will be particularly useful to readers who need information about the effects that various shoe design parameters have on the control of pronation and on cushioning. The precise data presented will help coaches, athletes, therapists, physicians, or podiatrists who are looking for certain stability and cushioning characteristics in a running shoe.

ACKNOWLEDGMENTS

In the process of putting this book together, I leaned so heavily on my colleague Peter Stipe as to feel guilty about not sharing the editorship with him. He and Elaine Bouchard deserve most of the credit and none of the blame, should any emerge, for the editorial work that went into the preparation of this volume.

E.C. Frederick

CHAPTER ONE

Load Sport Shoes and Playing Surfaces

Benno M. Nigg, J. Denoth, B. Kerr, S.Luethi, D. Smith, and A. Stacoff

The number of publications concerning biomechanical aspects of sport shoes and/or playing surfaces has proliferated since 1970, a fact which is perhaps due to reasons such as the following:

- Some manufacturers and researchers realize that pain and injuries connected with sports can be influenced by the variation of the materials and/or the construction of the shoe or the surface.
- The large increase in the number of joggers, tennis players, and other recreational sportsmen has resulted in an increasing number of specific injuries. One may assume that some of these negative effects may be partially influenced by sport shoes and/or surfaces. (Cavanagh & LaFortune, 1980).
- It may be that some of the most recent world records were facilitated by the types of shoes or sport surfaces.

This list of possibilities could perhaps be expanded. However, it is interesting to note that within the choice of possible criteria for sport shoe or playing surface construction, the criterion *load* has become important—a variable that can be quantified through biomechanical methods.

The research in this field has been primarily in the development of new methods of measurement (e.g., Cavanagh & Michiyoshi, 1980) or in the solution of applied problems. To the author's knowledge, however, a general overview concerning the factors that influence load has not yet been published. This publication will:

- Define "load" and expressions connected with it;
- Explain why load is a relevant parameter for sport shoe and playing surface construction;
- Give a general overview of the variables influencing load;
- Comment on some of the research conducted in this field during the past 10 years;
- Suggest some ideas for future development.

DEFINITION OF LOAD

Since the concept of load on the human body is not always used in the same way, the key terms are defined and explained.

Load

Load is defined as the external forces that act upon a body (in sport shoe and sport surface analysis, this is always the human body). Types of load include tension, compression, torsion, and shearing forces. Depending on the length of time involved, a distinction is made between *static* and *dynamic* load. Each material is limited in its capacity to bear force. The limit beyond which the material will be damaged is called the critical limit.

Load Capacity

Load capacity of an element is defined as the critical limit of the material. Load itself does not always have the same effect. A load with its line of action along the axis of a rod, for instance, generates a different pattern of stress than the same load with a line of action outside the axis. The tensile or compressive stresses may be many times higher in the nonaxial case than in the axial case. Analysis of load and effects of load therefore must take into consideration not only the magnitude of the acting forces, but also the geometry.

The human body is capable, to some degree, of actively adapting to external forces. The degree of adaptation may be connected with the frequency components in the acting forces. It is therefore useful to divide forces into high-frequency and low-frequency components. For this purpose, muscle latency (30 msec) serves to make the distinction. Following a signal, the muscles need approximately that much time or more before they can alter their state of tension. Therefore, one uses the expressions active and passive loading.

Active Load vs. Passive Load

In active load, the frequency is below 30 Hz. The muscles are able to change their state of tension actively while the force acts upon them. In passive load, the frequency is above 30 Hz. The muscles cannot voluntarily change their state of tension while the force acts upon them.

Active and passive loads are illustrated in Figure 1. The example demonstrates the vertical reaction force of a standing jump, with touchdown, on the heel of a sport shoe. A high frequency peak force is visible during landing. Otherwise, take-off and landing are nearly symmetrical, as shown in the lower part of the illustration. Such passive loads occur in human motion such as walking, running, and skipping.

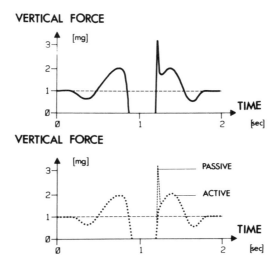

Figure 1   Illustration of the difference between active and passive load (two-legged standing jump with wind-up and landing on the heel). (mg = body weight)

LOAD AS A RELEVANT CRITERION FOR SPORT SHOE AND SPORT SURFACE CONSTRUCTION

Studies of load and the human body were initiated by the occurrence of pain as a result of various sport activities. Trainers and sport physicians

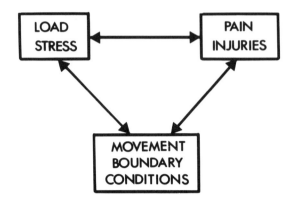

Figure 2   Schematic representation of the basic idea.

indicate that pain experienced by athletes in some portions of the musculo-skeletal system has increased during the past 20 years. According to Segesser (1976), 50% of the members of the Swiss middle and long distance team suffered pain in 1975. Analogous studies for subsequent years confirm these results. Several authors (Hess & Hort, 1973; Hort, 1976; Nigg et al., 1978; Prokop, 1976) relate such pains to external factors such as floors and sport shoes.

The research idea implicitly underlying all these studies is shown in Figure 2. Aspects to be studied include load, pain and injuries, as well as boundary conditions and movement. Since this contribution is mainly concerned with the issue of sport shoes and flooring, the boundary conditions to be considered in this review are the different types of sport shoes and flooring.

The use of load as a relevant parameter can be justified with the help of a study using tennis players. Over the past 20 years, hardly any sport has developed as vigorously as tennis. Formerly available only to the privileged few, tennis has now become a popular activity. Few other sports can boast of so many participants. Once an exclusively summer sport, tennis is now a year-round sport, thanks to the many indoor facilities having "artificial surfaces." But this development is paralleled by the increasing occurrence of pain, which may result from a single event (e.g., injury) or from frequent, repeated stress on one element of the musculoskeletal system. Tennis requires a specific playing area, and many tennis players play almost exclusively on one type of surface — at least for a season. Such a sport, then, permits us to gather information on the relationship between floor covering and the frequency of pain. Many other sports would make this type of data-gathering difficult because of constantly changing external conditions.

Therefore, to assess how the playing surface influences the frequency of pain sustained by tennis players, a survey questionnaire was distributed to 4,015 male and female tennis players (Nigg & Denoth, 1980). The questions concerned floor covering, racket (materials, size, and netting), game intensity, other sport activities, and type and location of pain and/or injuries. In addition, age, weight, and other individual data were also obtained. The information pertained only to winter 1978/79, summer 1979, and winter 1979/80. The grouping of floor coverings was determined by the texture of their respective surfaces.

In the evaluation, one test person per season was taken to be one case. Based on the information obtained, the following cases were excluded:

- individuals intensely pursuing other sports during the same season;
- individuals whose pain was obviously due to a cause other than the floor covering (e.g., the consequence of an earlier skiing injury);
- individuals who regularly played on several different types of floors during the same season.

Of the 4,015 questionnaires distributed, 3,915 were mailed and 100 deposited at the sport facilities; 1,018 (25.4%) were completed and returned. Presumably, many tennis players without impairments chose not to answer. This would imply that the percentage of those with impairments is higher in the sample than in the total population. However, it is assumed that the ratios per type of floor covering were not influenced.

Figure 3 shows the frequency of impairments of the lower extremities and of the back and pelvis. The data show the greatest frequen-

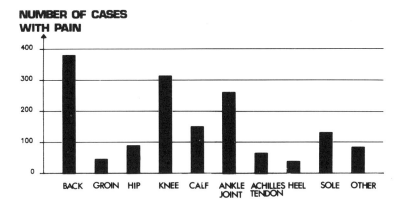

Figure 3   Frequency of pain in the lower extremities and in the back and pelvis regions.

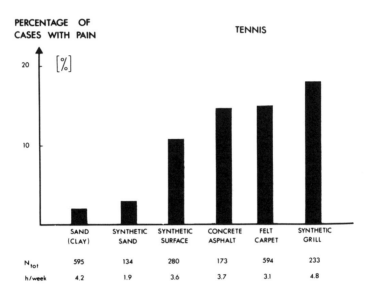

Figure 4 Relative frequency of surface related pain, by groups of floor covering.

cy for the back, the knee, and the ankle joint. So we will focus on these three types of impairments. Those in other parts of the body (e.g., arm, shoulder), which also occur frequently, will not be discussed. Frequency of pain did not seem related to age, but there seems to be a relationship between pain intensity and game intensity.

The central question in this survey was: Are there any differences in the frequency of pain which are a function of floor covering? In order to answer this, all cases were evaluated. It was found (Figure 4) that sand and synthetic sand (granular-synthetic floors) clearly relate to a lower percentage of pain than the floor groups of synthetic-solid, hard court, carpet, and synthetic mats. Sand and granular covers do not differ from one another.

The results suggest that the frequency of pain is connected with the type of surface. Since pain is a likely consequence of overloading, this indicates a possible correlation between load and surface. Similar results should be expected in analogous studies with sport shoes. The theoretical reflections, as well as the experimental results, show that load should be a relevant parameter in sport shoe as well as sport surface analysis.

The examples cited could lead to the conclusion that the effect of load on the human body is per se a negative one. However, it is well known that the absence of load upon the human system may lead to deficiencies (e.g., atrophy of bone tissue). Load does, indeed, have a stimulating effect upon the human body (Figure 5). It is essential to normal development of bone tissue, bone structure, and muscle cross-

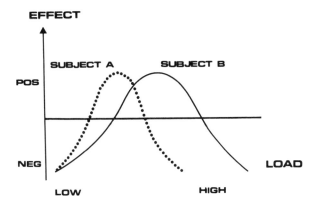

Figure 5 Schematic representation of the effect of load upon the human body for a given rate of loading.

section. For the elements of the human body, there is a zone in which load has a positive, i.e., stimulating, effect. Too little stress may have as negative an influence as too much stress. It should be noted, however, that individual stress curves (Figure 5) differ greatly.

In addition, some forces may have a *biopositive* effect in one part of the individual's organism while being *bionegative* in other parts. Physical discomfort may be one indication of excessive load on the musculo-skeletal system.

It follows that the load-bearing capacity of elements of the human body is not a constant value but is relative to the loading history. Moreover, it depends on age, nutrition, and so forth. Pain often occurs while changing from one surface type to another, such as during the transition from winter to summer training, or in changing from one type of shoe to another. If the change is done in stages, however, such pain often can be avoided.

VARIABLES INFLUENCING LOAD IN CONNECTION WITH SPORT SHOES AND SPORT SURFACES

If load is a relevant criterion in the analysis of sport shoes and sport surfaces, it is important to know the variables which influence load. This section is an attempt to develop and to illustrate a general schematic description of these variables (Figure 6).

Load is dependent on external influences, internal influences, and movement. ("First level" analysis.) External parameters are equipment (javelin, rucksack, etc.) and opponent (which will both be neglected in the following) as well as footwear and surface of the floor.

Internal factors are the anthropometric facts and the individual

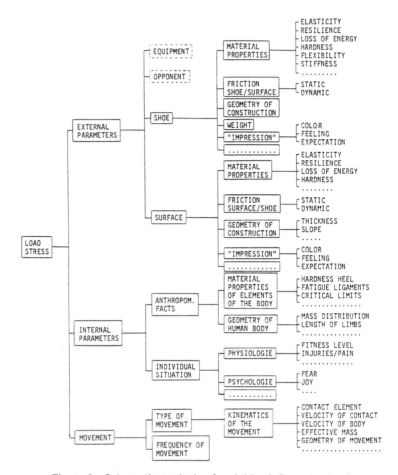

Figure 6   Schematic analysis of variables influencing load.

situation (from both a physiological and a psychological point of view). Movement may influence the load of the human body concerning the type of movement as well as the frequency of a certain type of movement. In the following, these "second level" variables will be discussed and illustrated with some experimental results.

Shoe and Surface

Since the structure of the influencing variables is similar for shoe and surface, the discussion will include both. Load may be influenced by the mechanical properties, the friction between shoe and surface, the geometry of construction of the shoe or surface, the weight of the shoe,

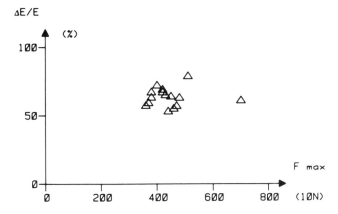

Figure 7   Relative energy loss δE/E and maximum brake force Fmax
in various samples of competition tracks. Drop test. (Height of drop:
20 cm; thickness of samples: 12-18 mm.)

the impression a subject gets from a shoe or surface, and other variables.

Material Properties.   Shoe and floor may be characterized by
certain material properties. The hardness of these materials, the loss of
energy, and so forth, is described in the dynamic case by stress-strain
diagrams. Such diagrams may be developed for homogeneous samples.
They also provide data on the elastic-plastic behavior of a given material.
Once the stress-strain information of the two materials is known, the corresponding values for their combination are also known.

In principle, energy loss and floor hardness are two independent
variables. A well-tended lawn is soft and rather plastic, whereas asphalt
is hard and "plastic." The energy loss of asphalt is irrelevant to an athlete, as he or she is hardly able to deform it. Synthetic flooring tends to
be hard and elastic: its hardness and energy loss are independent of one
another only to a degree—relative to its chemical makeup, the thickness
of the sample, and so forth. Figure 7 portrays the hardness and energy
loss of several flooring samples for competition facilities. It is assumed,
though not yet proven, that athletic achievement is related to energy loss,
and physical impairment to the hardness of a floor. It is easy to see that
synthetic floors can be produced which, while entailing approximately
the same energy loss, will vary greatly in hardness.

The hardness and energy loss of a floorcovering in a sport facility
cannot be determined by measuring only one spot, since the results vary
considerably from spot to spot. For example, up to 30% difference in the
maximum brake force has been noted for tracks 1 and 3 of some track
and field facilities. Other factors that should be considered in interpreting results include the following:

- Hysteresis: If, for example, a second measurement is taken in the same spot within an interval of about 5 seconds, the results will be influenced by the first impact (e.g., Fmax second reading about 10% greater than Fmax first reading). The data given in this paper consistently reflect first-impact readings.
- Temperature: Temperature also influences results!
- Maintenance: The results for lawns and cinder tracks depend on how well they are maintained.

The methods used for testing floors may also be used in testing shoes. However, it may be difficult to determine the hardness, energy loss, and stress-strain dependency of a complete shoe. The sole of the shoe is neither homogeneous nor isotropic. The heel of many sport shoes is filled with a foam material. The results therefore depend greatly on the choice of the area tested. Moreover, since the sole of the shoe is not usually smooth, the contact surface between sphere and sole is poorly defined.

For accurate interpretation of such results, each heel layer should be measured separately. Or vice versa: The tension-compression diagrams of the various materials and the desired conditions with respect to the function (of the entire shoe sole) permit theoretical determination of the composition of the sole.

Here and there, the opinion is expressed that statements regarding the load on the human kinetic system may be made entirely on the basis of data derived from materials tests. Such "theories" are dangerous, as materials tests can do no more than make a statement concerning properties of the material actually tested. However, it is useful to obtain,

TABLE 1   Sliding Friction Coefficients for Several Floor-Shoe Combinations Tested under Laboratory Conditions

Shoe	Surface				
	Carpet	Synthetic Granular	PVC	Sand	Asphalt
All round shoe little profile	1.05–1.15	0.95–1.05	1.00–1.20	0.40–0.60	0.70–0.80
Jogging shoe treaded profile	0.95–1.05	0.80–0.95	0.80–0.90	0.30–0.55	0.60–0.75
Tennis shoe indoor no profile	0.50–0.60	0.75–0.90	0.40–0.50	0.30–0.50	0.65–0.75

through materials tests, indications of the magnitude of parameters to be used in a model.

Friction. Sliding or nonsliding as well as rotation depend, among other considerations, upon surface properties. They are described by the static friction or sliding friction coefficient. For the purposes of estimates, Coulomb's Law of Friction, a law roughly verified by empirical means, will usually suffice. The static friction coefficient being independent of normal force is dependent only on the properties of the two contact surfaces. The sliding friction coefficient—slightly smaller than the static friction coefficient—is constant up to speeds of 10 m/sec.

The coefficients for static and sliding friction for several shoe-floor combinations are compiled in Tables 1 and 2. They were measured (Nigg & Denoth, 1980) at a normal force of 100 N and 225 N, and a contact surface of about 50 cm^2. Sliding speed ranged from 0.1 m/sec to 0.3 m/sec. On asphalt and sand, about 800 N normal force was additionally applied. The influence of normal force upon both the static and sliding friction coefficients is smaller in each case than the stated range.

Another method of gathering information about friction between surface and shoe is the measurement of the maximal torque exerted during a defined rotation. The maximal torque is connected with the static friction coefficient. Such measurements were performed (180 degrees rotation on one leg) with 12 subjects on 7 types of surface constructions with 8 different types of shoes. The mean values for the different types of floor surfaces are shown in Figure 8.

The results show large differences between the mean torques on the types of surfaces. They vary between about 20 Nm and 38 Nm. The torques measured are therefore roughly doubled on artificial grass

TABLE 2   Static Friction Coefficients for Several Floor-Shoe Combinations Tested under Laboratory Conditions

	Surface				
Shoe	Carpet	Synthetic Granular	PVC	Sand	Asphalt
All round shoe little profile	1.15–1.25	1.05–1.15	1.00–1.10	0.50–0.60	0.70–0.80
Jogging shoe treaded profile	1.05–1.15	0.95–1.05	0.80–0.90	0.40–0.60	0.70–0.80
Tennis shoe indoor no profile	0.60–0.70	0.80–0.90	0.40–0.50	0.40–0.50	0.75–0.85

MAXIMAL TORQUE

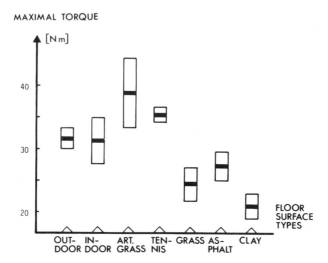

Figure 8   Mean values and standard errors for maximal torques in a defined horizontal rotation (180°) with sport shoes on different types of surfaces (12 subjects).

(astro-turf) in comparison to clay ("sand"). The same measurements were made for different types of shoes (basketball, tennis, and European handball) used in sports where rotation is important and occurs frequently. The results (Nigg & Denoth, 1980) show for these 8 shoes a variation of the mean values of the maximal torques between 28 Nm and 37 Nm. The results suggest that the human body is subjected to loads that vary considerably with the nature of the surface and/or the shoe involved. However, the unsolved problem connected with friction lies in the fact that too much friction as well as too little may have a negative effect on the human body.

Geometry of Construction.   The geometry of construction of a shoe or a surface may strongly influence the geometry of the movement, and therefore the load, of the human body. It is possible, for example, to influence the movement of the rearfoot somewhat with a medial support (Nigg, Luethi, Stacoff, & Segesser, 1981). Figure 9 shows results of such an experiment. Measurements were made on a basic shoe with and without medial support applied in four different positions from anterior to posterior, as well as barefoot. The illustrated parameter indicates the change of the "position of the calcaneus" in a 10th of the floor contact period (running with heel contact first) which corresponds in this example to about 30 msec. This time interval corresponds to the duration of the passive forces during landing.

The result shows that with this change in the geometry of the shoe, the pronation of the calcaneus (rearfoot control) can be influenced and it

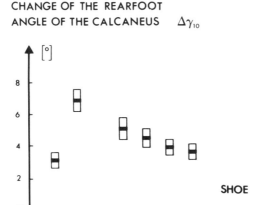

CHANGE OF THE REARFOOT
ANGLE OF THE CALCANEUS $\Delta\gamma_{10}$

Figure 9   Change of the angle of the heelbone $\delta\gamma_{10}$ (with standard error) in the first tenth of the floor contact period (pronation) for barefoot and footwear with different positions of the medial support.

suggests that the load on the different elements is therefore also altered. Other changes (e.g., construction of the heel) may even have great influence. They may influence the type of foot contact (heel, flat), the positioning of the foot and lower leg just before contact, and the movement during contact.

Other Influences.   Other factors may also influence the load on the human body. The weight of the shoe could have an influence. The impression a shoe or surface makes may influence load. Preliminary results suggest that the expectation one has of a shoe or a surface could change the movement pattern and therefore influence the load.

Anthropometric Facts

Material Properties of Elements of the Human Body.   The elements of the human body have material properties as do shoe parts and floor elements. In analogy to the force-deformation and stress-strain measurements described in the section on shoe and surface, measurements can be performed with the human heel. When measuring the heel, however, the method must be modified. The assumption is that the lower extremities may be replaced by rigid bodies with reduced mass. The test person sits on a chair and hits the platform dynamometer with his or her heel. Thus measured are reaction force, acceleration in the environment of epicondylus lateralis, and impact velocity. Assuming further that the heel approximates a sphere in shape, one may then determine the force-deformation or stress-strain diagrams as for point-elastic floors.

FORCE

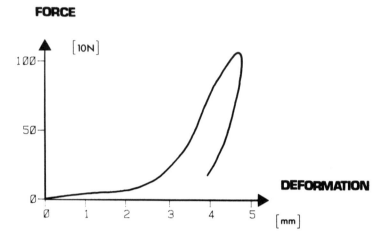

Figure 10 Force-deformation diagram for the heel of a subject (m = 50 kg, v = 1 m/sec).

The hardness of the heel is determined by the hardness of the ankle joint and of the tissue covering the calcaneus. The contact area, which is unknown, may be described by a mean radius. Force-deformation dependency and elasticity modulus can then be estimated. In a mature adult, the tissue over the calcaneus is about 10 mm thick. A typical force-deformation diagram for the heel of a test person is shown in Figure 10. There is a sharp bend in the force-deformation diagram. The level portion is due to the softness of the heel material and the size of the contact area. Once the material has been partly compressed, it becomes harder to deform and the curve therefore rises more steeply.

Analogous to floor and shoe, the actual hardness of the material can be described by tension-deformation diagrams. Figure 11 shows tension-deformation diagrams for 10 subjects. The precision of such measurements depends on the precision of the deformation reading (about 1 mm) and on the description of the heel by a sphere.

The foregoing remarks show that experimental determination of the tension-deformation diagrams for surface, shoe, and heel is feasible. An example will serve to illustrate this point (Figure 12).

In the configuration depicted, the surface is substantially harder than the shoe and the heel. If this is the case, the combined tension-deformation diagram for the floor-shoe-heel system derives chiefly from the properties of shoe and heel. If—as is the case in this example—the heel is softer than the shoe, it will become more deformed by a load than the shoe. Again, speaking about this example, two aspects may be distinguished. For small loads, shoe and heel are about equally soft, that is, they are deformed to approximately the same degree. For greater

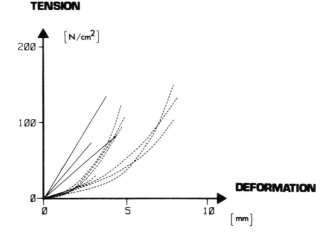

Figure 11   Tension-deformation diagrams for the heel of 10 subjects.

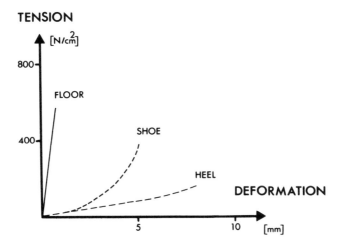

Figure 12   Schematic of a tension-deformation diagram for a floor, a shoe, and a heel.

loads (under which the shoe is completely compressed), the combined tension deformation diagram is primarily determined by the heel.

The general conclusion is that if the influence of floor, shoe, and heel upon passive loads in a vertical direction is to be determined, analysis of the tension-deformation diagram of floor, shoe, and heel is useful. This analysis will show which parts are deformed and to what degree. The diagram will also provide information on those load data which predominate for specific elements. For example, if the passive loads during heel contact (given shoe, heel, and movement pattern) are to be reduced by 50% compared to asphalt, the tension-deformation diagrams of shoe and heel will permit determination of the floor properties required to achieve this end. Analogous considerations can be made for the shoe.

If material properties of elements of the human body are discussed, it would be important to have information about critical limits of the different elements in the human body. To determine the limits of loading, we can use the critical values for human tissues determined by Yamada (1973). Yamada reported that critical pressure for cartilage is 500 N/cm^2 (a critical value is one beyond which structural damage will occur to the tissue). With an estimated congruent area of the knee joint of about 4 cm^2, the critical force would be about 2000 N, a value that is exceeded in many human movements. This example shows that such figures for "critical limits" of elements of the human body should be used with caution (Viidik, 1980). In addition, it demonstrates that general limits cannot be determined with the knowledge currently available (Baumann & Stucke, 1980). As a consequence of this, there is not enough information available at this time to permit the development of norms and standards.

Geometry of the Human Body. It is evident that the geometry of the human body strongly influences the load of the human body. Different length and proportion of limbs, different mass distribution, and other anthropometrical facts are connected with individual movement patterns and may therefore influence loading of the human body.

INDIVIDUAL SITUATION

A person's individual situation may also influence the loading on the body. Psychological situations such as joy or fear may change movement pattern and therefore influence the loading of various elements of the body. An example of this was analyzed and reported as follows.

The movement of the feet of 45 normal subjects and of 10 subjects with weaknesses in their fibulotalar and fibulocalcaneal ligaments were filmed (posterior view). Analyzed were the position of the calcaneus, masked with two markers at the heel of the shoe, and the position of the Achilles tendon, masked with two other markers on the skin. The results are depicted in Figure 13 and show that the change in the angle of the calcaneus (rearfoot angle) $\Delta\gamma_{10}$ in the first 10th of floor contact and the correspondent value for the angle of the Achilles tendon as well as the total pronation and supination of the heel $\Delta\gamma_{tot}$ are different for subjects with weaknesses in their ligaments than for normal subjects.

This difference may be a consequence of the weaknesses, or the

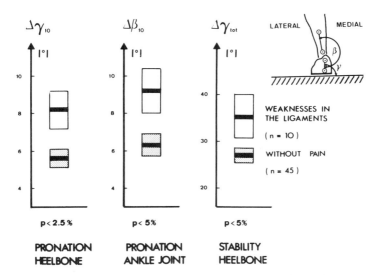

Figure 13 Change and standard error of the angle of the calcaneus $\delta\gamma_{10}$, the Achilles tendon $\delta\beta_{10}$ during the first tenth of foot contact and total pronation and supination of the heel $\delta\gamma_{tot}$ for subjects with weaknesses in the fibulotalar and fibulocalcaneal ligaments in comparison with normal subjects.

weaknesses could be a result of the different movements. The measurements on subjects with pain or injuries do not reveal the cause or the results. The origin of pain can only be derived from analyzing healthy subjects and then reanalyzing them if they later develop pain. However, the results show that there is a difference in the movement pattern for different individual situations (pain/normal) and it is assumed that the different movement means a different loading on the elements of the musculoskeletal system.

TYPE OF MOVEMENT

Determining the load sustained by the human body on various surfaces or with various shoes is possible only if the behavior of these surfaces or shoes is also known. Comparison of passive forces in the ankle and knee joints require identical preliminary conditions. However, it has been shown that floor and shoe cause a change in movement, that is, the test person will adapt to the flooring or shoe. Extreme differences are encountered in playing tennis on sand courts and hard courts. But even in running, the movement is relative to the surface. This type of movement may change (toe contact/heel contact). Some individuals change gait ac-

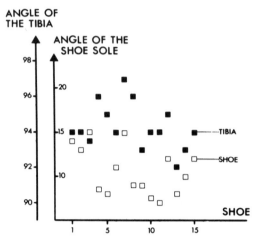

Figure 14   Results of the angle of the tibia, the angle of the shoe sole, both immediately before contact and type of first floor contact for one test subject running on a treadmill (v = 3 m/sec).

cording to the surface they are running on. Moreover, some individuals will make initial heel contact on all surfaces while jogging, running, or sprinting, whereas others run only on the forefoot without making heel contact at all.

The analysis of one subject running with 15 different types of so-called high quality (= expensive) jogging shoes should illustrate this. Three different parameters were studied: the angle of the tibia to the medial side (frontal view), the angle of the shoe sole to the ground (rear view), both just before contact, and the type of first foot contact.

Figure 14 shows that there are remarkable differences between these 15 shoes in the measured parameters. The angle of the tibia varies between 92 and 97 degrees, the angle of the shoe sole between 7 and 15 degrees! Even different shoes from the same company show large differences. Company X has differences in the shoe sole angle of 8 degrees, company Y, 6 degrees, and so forth. The test subject also changed the type of first contact; with 10 shoes the first contact was with the heel, whereas in the other 5 it was with a flat foot (along the lateral edge from heel to midsole).

When an individual runs on the forefoot, an additional joint is called into action at the point of touchdown. As a result, the reaction forces on the ground differ greatly between toe contact and heel contact. Passive load on the ankle and knee joints is significantly greater during heel contact than during toe contact. There are also notable differences in the Achilles tendon. During the touchdown phase, the Achilles tendon is, at most, loaded by lateral stability functions when the heel touches the

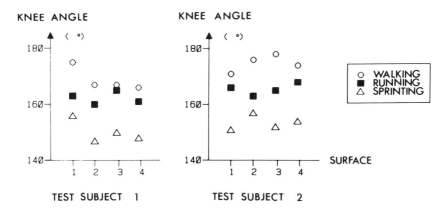

Figure 15   Mean values for knee angles, at initial heel contact, of two test persons walking, running, and sprinting.

ground. But when only the forefoot touches the ground, it experiences significant tensile load (about 2 to 10 times the individual's weight).

With a certain gait (e.g., heel contact), the touchdown velocity and knee angle change — at the moment of initial heel contact — are a function of the floor surface. It is as yet unknown whether general reactive rules do exist. But even if they do, individual variation is rather great. An example of the knee angle of two test persons on four different surfaces should illustrate this (Figure 15). The tests are performed barefoot. The floor coverings are rated 1 to 4 according to hardness (1 being very hard, 4 very soft).

The test person on the left, when touching ground, flexes the knee less if the floor is harder. As a result, the passive loads are increased during touchdown, as the accelerated (effective) mass is greater. If one were to look at only the knee angle, it would appear that the test person is making a mistake. But in fact, the individual is trying to reduce load via touchdown velocity. On the hard floor he/she makes ground contact about half as rapidly as on the soft floor. The test person on the right maintains approximately the same touchdown velocity for all floors, reacting to the various degrees of hardness by changing the knee angle; the tendency is that the angle tends to be smaller for hard floors.

The results for these two test persons imply that one generally attempts to reduce load but that the manner in which one does this differs for each individual.

Because in many cases it is difficult or even impossible to measure the force in a certain element of the human body, substantial methods were developed to describe the movement. A film analysis method was presented by Nigg and co-workers in 1978. The method uses film from the posterior view (Figure 16).

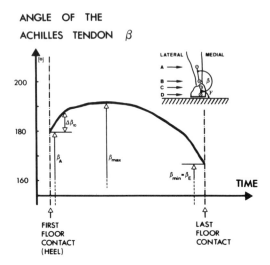

Figure 16   Schematic illustration of the film analysis method with posterior view.

This method provides information on pronation and supination of the foot as well as information on positioning of the lower leg and foot. It seems plausible that the Achilles tendon angle and the heelbone angle are connected with the loading of the foot's ligaments. However, it still has to be proved that this parameter really is relevant in the analysis of loading the ligaments of the foot.

FREQUENCY OF MOVEMENT

It is evident that the frequency of a certain movement may have an influence on the loading of the human body. Long-distance running will serve to illustrate such periodic forces. The musculoskeletal system of a marathon runner, who takes about 30,000 steps in one run, experiences passive loads at each ground contact. They act upon bones, ligaments, tendons, muscles, and so forth. A comparison of this number with the critical limit of steel shows that these orders of magnitudes are not far different from one another!

CRITICAL COMMENTS AND SOME IDEAS

A review of the literature on sport shoes and sport floors leads to a possible grouping of research and measurements performed in the last 10 years:

1. Studies that mainly emphasize the measuring technique inside and outside the shoe;
2. Studies of a mainly descriptive character using one of these methods or techniques;
3. Studies of a dogmatic character, setting criteria for qualities of shoes or surfaces;
4. Studies with an analytical emphasis, trying to understand the mechanism and origin of load, overload, and resulting pain as well as performance and energy in connection with shoe or surface.

Most of the publications known by the author are in categories 1, 2, and 3. A basic understanding of how sport shoes and playing surfaces should be constructed in order to reduce load will be gained primarily with analytical analysis. The following example should illustrate this.

It is a fact that some subjects run with heel-toe and others with toe contact. The difference in the loading of a certain element of the musculoskeletal system can be determined by modeling this part of the body in a way that the key elements are present and the simplified version represents a mechanical system. This system permits deduction of measurable substitute values describing the desired values (Nigg & Denoth, 1980). By measuring these substitute values, we can determine the loading of the element of interest of the musculoskeletal system. However, the question remains as to why some people run with heel-toe and others only with forefoot contact.

An experiment done on the treadmill can help answer this question. One skilled test subject ran on the treadmill in his own running shoes. The treadmill speed was increased 0.44 m/s every 50 seconds during the continuous run. Oxygen consumption and the angle of the shoe sole (lateral view) were measured. The idea was that slow speed movements usually result in heel contact movements whereas fast running or sprinting is usually with forefoot contact at touchdown. Somewhere in between is a change from a positive to a negative foot angle (discontinuity). Is this influenced by energy? Figure 17 shows the result for one test subject. The change from a positive foot angle (heel contact) to a negative one (forefoot contact) is at a speed of about 5 m/sec. Up to this velocity, oxygen consumption increases linearly as expected. Shortly before the change from heel to toe running, oxygen consumption begins to level off. The subject may have reached his energy potential for this style. He may have changed his running style, due to a change in metabolism with in-

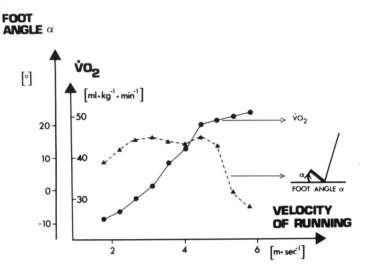

Figure 17   Type of foot contact (heel/toe) and energy consumption for different running speeds.

creasing speed (i.e., rapid increase in anaerobiosis) in order to maintain or increase the running speed.

Looking at such an experiment may lead to other speculations. (a) It may be that heel or toe running are determined by energy demands. The human body may unconsciously choose the solution that consumes less energy. That is, a person who runs on toes may be doing so for energy reasons. (b) It may be that some athletes run with a certain style not because of energy consideration but because of information from a coach. The comparison between the two oxygen consumption values could give information in this connection. (c) Since shoe and surface influence and sometimes change the movement patterns (heel/toe), it may be interesting for the shoe manufacturer to know of these changes and that they also are related to energy considerations. (d) If movement patterns change, it is assumed that the load distribution changes too. It may be that certain changes of style occur not only because of energy reasons but also because of protection of some elements of the musculoskeletal system.

The list of speculations could be expanded. However, the example shows that a combination of descriptive and analytic approaches may serve as a basis for understanding shoe and surface construction.

The schematic analysis described in Figure 6 does not show the intercorrelation between the variables in the same level (column). These are important, however, and further studies are needed in order to analyze how these variables are connected.

ACKNOWLEDGMENT

This paper summarizes research performed by Biomechanics Laboratory of ETH Zurich, Switzerland, and the Centre of Human Performances Studies, University of Calgary, Canada, concerning sport shoes and playing surfaces. The research was performed over the past 8 years and is a result of the teamwork of both groups. However, special mention should be made of the outstanding contribution by Dr. J. Denoth of the Biomechanics Laboratory of ETH Zurich.

REFERENCES

Baumann, W., and Stucke, H. Sportspezifische Belastungen aus der Sicht der Biomechanik (Loading in sport from a biomechanical point of view). In: Cotta, Krahl, and Steinbrueck: *Die Belastungstoleranz des Bewegungsapparates*. Georg Thieme, Stuttgart, 1980, pp. 58-64.

Cavanagh, P.R., and Lafortune, M.A. Ground reaction forces in distance running. *J. Biomechanics* **13**:397-406, 1980.

Cavanagh, P.R., and Michiyoshi, A. A technique for the display of pressure distributions beneath the foot. *J. Biomechanics* **13**:69-75, 1980.

Hess, H., and Hort, W. Erhoehte Verletzungsgefahr beim Leichtathletik training auf Kunststoffboeden (Increased danger of injuries on artificial track and field sport surfaces). *Sportarzt und Sportmedizin* **12**:282-285, 1973.

Hort, W. Ursachen, Klinik, Therapie und Prophylaxe der Schaeden auf Leichtathletik-Kunststoffbahnen (Origin, clinics, therapy and prevention of injuries caused by artificial track and field sport surfaces). *Leistungssport* **1**:48-52, 1976.

Nigg, B.M., and Denoth, J. *Sportplatzbelage* (Playing surfaces). Juris Verlag, Zurich, 1980.

Nigg, B.M., Eberle, G., Frey, D., Luethi, S., Segesser, B., and Weber, B. Gait analysis and sportshoe construction. In: Asmussen and Joergensen, *Biomechanics VIA*, University Park Press, Baltimore, 1978, pp. 303-309.

Nigg, B.M., Luethi, S., Stacoff, A., and Segesser, B. Biomechanical effects of pain and sportshoe corrections. *Australian Sports Biomechanics Lecture Tour*, 1981.

Prokop, L. Sportmedizinsche Probleme der Kunststoffbelaege (Medical sports problems caused by artificial floor surfaces). *Sportstaettenbau und Baederanlagen* **4**:1175-1181, 1976.

Segesser, B. Die Belastung des Bewegungsapparates auf Kunststoffboeden (Loading of the human body on artificial surfaces). *Sportstaettenbau und Baederanlagen* **4**:1183-1194, 1976.

Viidik, A. Elastomechanik biologischer Gewebe (Elastomechanics of biological tissue). In: Cotta, Krahl, and Steinbrueck: *Die Belastungstoleranz des Bewegungsapparates*. George Thieme, Stuttgart, 1980, pp. 124-136.

Yamada, H. *Strength of biological material*. R.E. Krieger, Huntington, NY, 1973.

CHAPTER TWO

Biological Aspects of Modeling Shoe/Foot Interaction During Running

P.R. Cavanagh, G.A. Valiant, and K.W. Misevich

Any model of the interaction between the shoe, the foot, and the ground must depend for its validity not only on the equations used to define the system, but also on the various constants and initial conditions that govern the behavior of the model. This paper attempts to provide a summary of such data both from the existing literature and from experiments conducted specifically for this project.

A number of studies in the literature pertain to shoe-ground interaction but there is very little data on the interaction between the foot and the shoe. Neither are the mechanical properties of the foot well documented. For example, while many authorities acknowledge the importance of the subcalcaneal fat pad as a biological shock absorber (Kuhns, 1949), there is little experimental work describing its structure and function.

This paper will address the following areas:

1. Delimitation;
2. Landing kinematics;
3. Ground reaction forces;
4. Center of pressure;
5. Heel properties;
6. In-shoe pressure measurements.

These last five areas together comprise a significant proportion of the total sum of knowledge needed to specify realistic values for the various parameters incorporated into a model of shoe/foot/ground interactions.

DELIMITATION

The initial contact between the foot and the ground has often in the past been termed "heel strike." It is important to state here our belief that "foot strike" is a far more appropriate term. Center of pressure measurements (Cavanagh & LaFortune, 1980) have shown that, even at fairly slow running speeds, many people make first contact between the shoe and the ground in some region other than the heel or rear part of the shoe. Classifying individuals according to this first point of contact using a "strike index" (Cavanagh, 1980, p. 89) has led to the terms rearfoot striker, midfoot striker, and forefoot striker to identify which region of the shoe first makes contact with the ground.

To calculate the strike index, a perpendicular is drawn from the shoe midline to the point on the shoe border where the center of pressure path first enters the outline. The distance along the midline from the heel to this perpendicular is then expressed as a percentage of shoe length. Thus, the strike index would be 33% for a runner whose first point of contact, as determined by the center of pressure pattern, was one-third of the way along the shoe midline from the heel. This is illustrated in Figure 1.

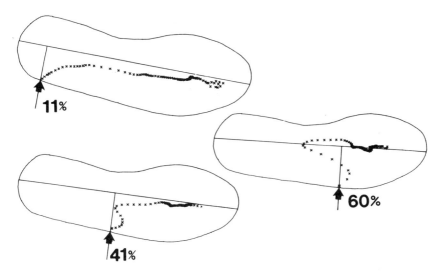

Figure 1   Strike index calculation from the center of pressure patterns of three different runners.

In light of the foregoing discussion, it should be noted that the analysis in this and the accompanying paper (Misevich & Cavanagh, in press) only apply to individuals who would be classified as rearfoot strikers. Many individuals never contact the ground with their heel during level running, and although the same general principles could apply to an analysis of their ground contact, due consideration would have to be given to the anatomical and material properties of the strike region of the foot and the shoe.

LANDING KINEMATICS

To determine the kinematics of the shoe's approach to the ground, high-

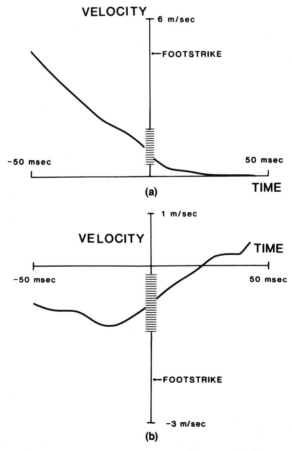

Figure 2 Mean velocity component of the heel marker from 10 different rearfoot strikers running at 3.6 m/s. (a) horizontal; (b) vertical.

speed cinematography was used to analyze the shoe motion at footstrike of 10 rearfoot strikers running in a straight line at 3.6 meters per second. Targets were placed on the lateral malleolus and on the midsole of the heel, adjacent to the base of the fifth metatarsal and the tip of the fifth toe. After smoothing the digitized data with a three-point moving average, finite difference techniques were used to derive horizontal and vertical components of velocity.

As shown by the shaded bar in Figure 2a, there was considerable spread about the mean of +0.90 meters per second in the horizontal component of the velocity of the heel target at foot strike among 10 subjects. However, all subjects displayed a forward velocity component indicating the scuffing nature of the foot's landing on the ground. This finding is further reinforced by the fact that the mean curve continues to show a forward directed velocity vector for some time after first contact.

The mean value of the vertical component of velocity at footstrike in this group of subjects was −0.70 meters per second with a range from −0.16 to −1.20 meters per second. The curve shown in Figure 2b also indicates that there is no real dwell period at zero vertical velocity for the heel target—an upward component immediately follows the negative velocity phase.

Figure 3 summarizes the mean results for all subjects of the resultant velocity vectors for all points on the shoe at the instant of footstrike. Because of the plantar flexion that usually accompanies footstrike in a rearfoot striker, the vertical velocity components of the markers on the front part of the shoe are considerably greater than that of the heel at the time of first ground contact.

The data in Figures 2 and 3 indicate that an impact velocity of ap-

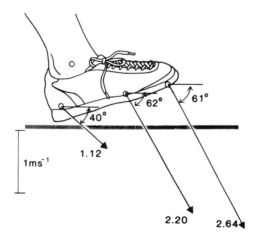

Figure 3 Mean resultant velocities at foot strike of shoe markers from 10 rearfoot strikers running at 3.6 ms⁻¹.

proximately 1.1 meters per second (±0.41) would be appropriate in a laboratory simulation that attempted to reproduce the heel impact conditions of running at 3.6 meters per second.

GROUND REACTION FORCES (GRF)

Ground reaction forces during distance running have been described in detail by Cavanagh and Lafortune. Figure 4 shows two fundamentally different patterns for the vertical component of the GRF in rearfoot strikers and others. While both curves show peak values of approximately three times body weight at the time of mid-support, the rearfoot strikers exhibit an initial peak early in the contact phase that is not usually found in those who contact the ground with the mid and forefoot regions. It is this first peak that is of major concern in the present study since, as we shall later see, this represents the peak stress in the rearfoot region.

For the purpose of modeling, it is instructive to consider the vertical component of the GRF as a composite of the two schematic curves shown in Figure 5. Of interest to this study is the initial curve, with a peak approximately 2.9 times body weight and a time to peak of approximately 25 milliseconds. An impulse of these characteristics would be an appropriate impact to the heel or to the rear part of the shoe to simulate the footstrike in distance running. Indeed, these values have been used to determine the drop height of a missile in a drop test of shoe materials and to control the crosshead movement of an INSTRON in a simulation to the drop test (Misevich & Cavanagh, in press). The second curve, with a

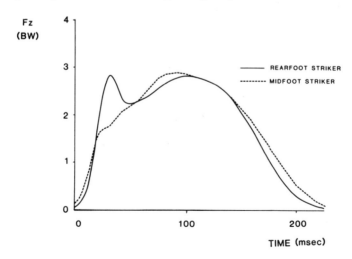

Figure 4 Vertical component of ground reaction force (Fz) vs time for a rearfoot and a midfoot striker.

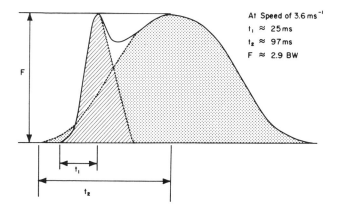

At Speed of 3.6 ms^{-1}

$t_1 \approx 25\,ms$

$t_2 \approx 97\,ms$

$F \approx 2.9\,BW$

Figure 5 Two schematic segments of an Fz vs time curve for a rear-foot striker.

similar peak and considerably longer rise time would serve as a useful model for studying the loading history of other regions of the foot and shoe in a rearfoot striker.

Force platform studies and intuition concerning the braking phase of ground contact suggest that there is more than just a compressive component to the resultant GRF during the early phase of ground contact. A typical resultant force vector at the time of the first peak in the vertical component of the GRF is shown projected onto sagittal and frontal planes in Figure 6. These figures indicate that the mediolateral component of the GRF results in minimal deviation of the resultant force vector from the vertical when viewed in a frontal plane but that the anteposterior component is large enough to cause a deviation of approximately 7 degrees from the vertical in the sagittal plane. The tissues of the foot and the materials of the shoe outsole and midsole will therefore be

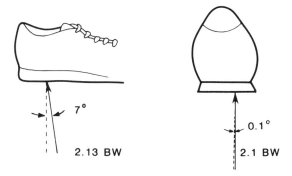

7°

2.13 BW

0.1°

2.1 BW

Figure 6 The resultant GRF vector in the sagittal and frontal planes at foot strike.

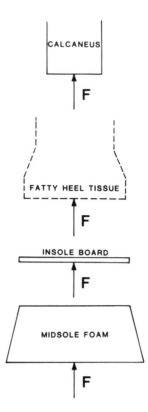

Figure 7 The net forces are equal in a composite at all levels.

subject to some shear stress as well as compressive stress. Thus, the use of only a compressive stress in the current model (Misevich & Cavanagh, 1983) is acknowledged to be a first order approximation to the actual force environment of the foot and shoe.

We should mention here the obvious but sometimes forgotten axiom that net forces at all levels of the ground/shoe/foot system are exactly equal to those measured at the ground. This point, illustrated in Figure 7, means that the shoe manufacturer cannot change the net forces that exist simply by changing the materials in the shoe (although the subject may change his or her movement pattern in different shoes, thereby modifying the GRF). Different shoes can modify the pressures that exist at the various levels and thus they can modify the effects of the applied force on the foot or the shoe material.

CENTER OF PRESSURE (C of P)

It is a fairly straightforward procedure to obtain a record of the migra-

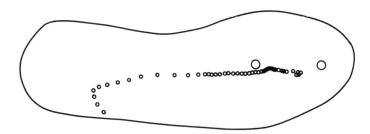

Figure 8 Mean center of pressure plot for the 10 rearfoot strikers mentioned in Figures 1-4 running at 3.6 m/s.

tion of the center of pressure under the shoe or under the bare foot during contact with the ground in running. A typical record for a rearfoot striker is shown in Figure 8. An outline of the shoe has been drawn in a single location, although in most subjects the foot moves to some extent during ground contact. It is apparent that the center of pressure path never actually passes under what might be considered from anatomical speculation to be the actual weight-bearing area of the heel (under the medial and lateral tuberosities of the calcaneus).

Conversely, the center of pressure path shown in Figure 9 (from a single subject walking) passes through regions where there can be no weight-bearing because the foot has such a high arch that no contact with the ground is possible.

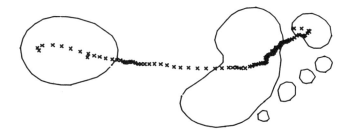

Figure 9 Center of pressure plot taken during walking from a subject with a cavus foot.

Both of these phenomena are expressions of the major limitation of the center of pressure for the purposes of insight into shoe design—namely that it is an averaging technique which yields a single point to represent a complex and potentially multidimensional pressure distribution. Complete insight can only be gained by determining the characteristics of the entire pressure distribution and not simply some average of it. Another limitation of the C of P is that it is a function of the pressure distribution between the shoe and the ground, which is not the principal interface of interest.

It would be wrong, however, to convey the impression that the C of P is a measure that has no utility in an overall description of the contact phase. For example, right/left asymmetry can clearly be demonstrated using center of pressure measurement and the concept of strike index mentioned earlier is another useful measure derived from the C of P.

HEEL PROPERTIES

Anatomical Characteristics

When examining the biological structures involved in the foot/shoe/ground interaction, it is appropriate to look first at the calcaneus or heel bone. From the medial view shown in Figure 10a, it is clear that the primary structures involved in the transmission of rear foot loads in the normal foot (the calcaneal tuberosities) have a remarkable small cross section in the sagittal plane. Moving anteriorly, the rough ridge of the tuberosity is soon undercut by the arch to the anterior tubercle.

A posterior view (Figure 10b) indicates that it is incorrect to describe the profile of the inferior surface of the calcaneus as spherical. There are actually two small prominences, one medial and one lateral, with a ridge of variable height between them. Despite the fact that calcaneii from different individuals vary a great deal in their shapes, there is enough species similarity to allow anthropologists to use profiles of fossil foot bones to infer the locomotor characteristics of the species from which the bone was derived (Day & Napier, 1966).

Turning now to the soft tissue, the partially dissected cadaver foot shown in Figure 11 reveals the presence of an extensive fat pad between the calcaneus and the cutaneous tissues. Anecdotal evidence from surgeons who have dissected the fat pad in the living subject indicate that there is a major difference between this region and most other regions with large deposits of adipose tissue in the body. Upon incision, the fatty

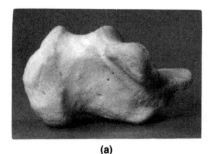 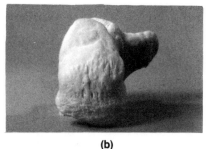

(a)   (b)

Figure 10   Left calcaneus. (a) medial view; (b) posterior view.

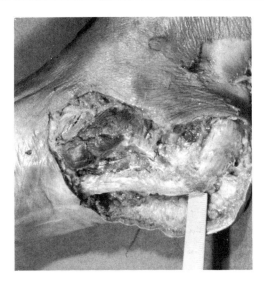

Figure 11   Partial dissection of a right foot to show the extent of the subcalcaneal fat pad.

tissue will "burst" from its attachments, suggesting that a positive "compartmental" type of pressure exists in the region.

Histological Appearance

Histological studies of the subcalcaneal fat pad have indeed shown it to be a highly specialized structure. The region is characterized by the presence of a matrix of connective tissue (elastic fibrous tissue) arranged in septa containing closely packed fat cells (Kuhns, 1949). Blechschmidt (1933) studied tissue from human embryos, stating that these gave an undistorted representation of the structure. He described U-shaped (in sec-

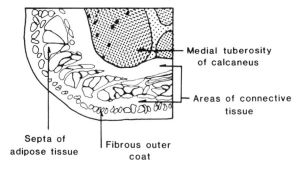

Figure 12   Schematic diagram of normal elastic adipose tissue and the fibrous stroma from the heel of a child (redrawn from 7).

tion) connective tissue strands tied down at the open end to the calcaneus. Transverse and diagonal strands of elastic fibers completed a compartment filled with fat cells. Blechshmidt commented on the spiral arrangement of fibrous tissue within the compartments as a mechanism for binding the fat cells together. This arrangement is shown schematically in Figure 12 redrawn from his micrographs.

Clinical Findings

Curiously, much of our knowledge concerning the dimensions of the fat pad in living subjects is due to the fact that thickening in this region is one of the first detectable signs of the chronic disease, acromegaly. Steinbach and Russell (1964) performed soft tissue heel X-rays on normal subjects and on patients with acromegaly. Their results, summarized in Figure 13, showed the mean thickness of the heel pad in Caucasian controls to be 17.8 mm. American blacks in the study had a 2.3 mm greater thickness than the symptom-free Caucasian group. These thicknesses are much greater than would be imagined by simply palpating the heel region of a living subject because the fat pad rapidly stiffens upon compression. It is therefore somewhat surprising to learn that there is approximately the same thickness of uncompressed adipose tissue under the calcaneus as there is foam material in the rear part of the running shoe. It is clear that this biological shock absorber should be given as much consideration as the mechanical shock absorption the shoe provides.

The lack of regeneration of the heel pad following serious injury or surgical insult has also been mentioned by a number of authors. Although Kuhns (1949) states that a certain amount of repair may occur in cases of mild degeneration, he points out that in severe crushing injuries that involve the blood supply, the elastic adipose tissue remains permanently incompetent. Most surgical procedures involving the plantar aspect of the calcaneus involve a medial or lateral approach. The domi-

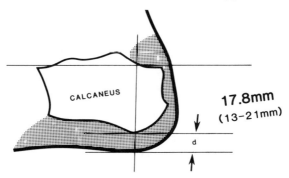

Figure 13   Mean heel pad thickness for Caucasians (taken from 8).

nant philosophy appears to be that expressed by Miller (1982), who states, "the heel pad must be retained at all costs since it is so highly differentiated and cannot be reformed after damage."

Another interesting property of the heel pad gained from clinical studies is the observation that the body jealously guards the adipose tissue stored in the heel during times of nutritional adversity. Batty Shaw (1902) and Wells (1940) have noted that fat cells from the heel pad are spared from nutritional metabolism "for a long time" during periods of fasting.

Mechanical Properties

There have been few attempts to characterize the mechanical properties of the heel tissue. Nigg and Denoth (1980) present stress-deformation diagrams for presumably single trials in 10 subjects. The authors offer few details of the experimental procedures, and it is unclear how measurements of stress were obtained from a contact area that is rapidly changing and difficult to measure. At similar reported stress levels of 100 $N \cdot cm^{-2}$, deformations of between 2.5 and 8 mm were reported. Three of the subjects exhibited linear relationships between stress and deformation over the whole of the measured range while the remaining subjects showed nonlinear curves, increasing in stiffness with increasing loads. In a separate report by Denoth and Nigg (1981), a load deformation curve from a single subject is presented showing a stiffness of 10^5 $N \cdot m^{-1}$ at low loads and a value of 1.5×10^6 $N \cdot m^{-1}$ at the higher loads.

The objectives of our own experimental work in this area are as follows:

1. To provide a reliable and reproducible method to measure certain mechanical properties of the heel under impact conditions similar to those that occur in running;
2. To obtain estimates of energy dissipation by the heel;
3. To examine the variation in the above in a group of subjects;
4. To study the effects of repeated impacts on stiffness and energy absorption;
5. To examine the pattern of tissue displacement in the heel at impact;
6. To derive a model that satisfactorily accounts for some of the above phenomena.

A full discussion of all these factors is clearly beyond the scope of the present report, but the major results will be summarized here.

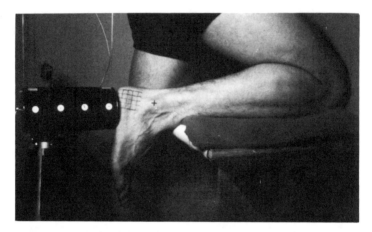

Figure 14 Experimental arrangement for the heel impact tests showing the ballistic pendulum, photocell and subject with femoral condyles firmly against wall.

After a number of unsuccessful initial experimental arrangements were rejected, the ballistic pendulum shown in Figure 14 was constructed. It consisted of a mass of 1.9 kg (with provision for the attachment of additional weights) suspended by 1.22-meter long nylon cords from an overhead beam. The impact surface was a flat 8.8-cm diameter circular aluminum plate with an accelerometer mounted in the mass. The output of the accelerometer was sampled at 20 kHz by an analog to digital converter triggered by photocells just prior to impact. The velocity at impact was calculated from the change in potential energy of the impact mass, assuming negligible losses and zero vertical velocity component at impact. The displacement of the impact mass was calculated by double integration of the acceleration-time record using the velocity at impact as an initial condition.

From the data on landing kinematics presented earlier, a value close to 1 $m \cdot sec^{-1}$ (actually 1.03 $m \cdot sec^{-1}$) was chosen as the impact velocity for the pendulum during the heel impacting experiments. At this velocity a mass of 4 kg represented the upper limit of subject tolerance to the impact. Therefore, masses between 1.9 and 4.0 kg were used in the experiments. This resulted in input energies that varied from 2.96 J to 4.26 J.

Double-exposure strobe photographs were taken with the first exposure at the instant of impact and the second close to the time of maximum penetration (as estimated from a previous impact under the same conditions). High speed cinematography was also employed in representative trials to verify the impact velocity and to measure displacement of the leg during the impact.

The subjects were placed, as shown in Figure 14, with the femoral condyles firmly against a rigid wall. This minimized the leg movements that were included in the total measure of deformation during impact. Cine measurements confirmed that only small displacements (approximately 2 to 3 mm) of the leg occurred relative to a fixed external reference frame.

Table 1 summarizes the results from impacts on 10 subjects with a mass of 1.90 kg at a velocity of 1.03 m·sec^{-1}. The peak accelerations recorded were rather high (mean 20.8 G, sd 3.5 G) but because the impacting mass was only 1.9 kg the peak forces were actually less than one body weight. It was mentioned earlier that an impacting mass of twice this value brought the subject to the threshold of pain. The relatively low forces encountered are an indication that an impact with a flat plate does not match the pressure distribution conditions that occur in the shoe — since pain is not experienced during a typical impact during running. Approximately 85% of the input energy was absorbed during the impact, suggesting that a fairly effective shock absorber is present. It is clear that this energy absorption is partitioned between the heel/foot/leg system in a manner that cannot be separated in the present experiment.

Table 1 also shows that the average peak deformation of the heel after impact is approximately 1 cm — a fairly large value when one considers how quickly the heel hardens upon palpation. These calculated values for heel deformation were confirmed directly by double-exposure strobe photographs such as that shown in Figure 15. The first exposure was triggered by electrical contact between the pendulum and a conducting strip on the heel and thus represents the instant of initial contact. The second exposure was made at a time, t, after initial contact where t was estimated from previous trials under identical conditions to be the time to peak acceleration. The two white horizontal lines in Figure 15 are the two exposures of the head of the pendulum, and their separation therefore indicates pendulum displacement from initial contact to peak acceleration. The parallel lines drawn over the Achilles tendon, which are 1 cm apart, show that there has been very little movement of the foot in a cranial direction. The small circles on the posterior aspect of the heel have been displaced in both medial and lateral directions.

TABLE 1   The Effect of Two Different Initial Velocities of the Pendulum on Various Measured Parameters

	Velocity 1.03 m·s^{-1}	Velocity 1.44 m·s^{-1}
Peak acceleration	20.8 G	36.3 G
Peak force	338 N	676 N
Energy absorbed	85 %	90 %
Max deformation	8.8 mm	10.9 mm
"Permanent" deformation	5.1 mm	7.0 mm

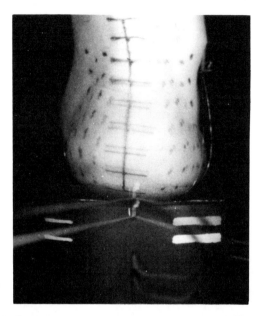

Figure 15 Double exposure photograph showing the posterior surface of the heel and a top view of the pendulum. The first exposure was taken at the instant of impact, the second at approximately the time of peak acceleration. See text for further details.

Since continuous data for force and deformation were available throughout the impact, force-deformation curves were plotted in a similar manner to previous investigators (Denoth & Nigg, 1981; Nigg & Denoth, 1980). Figure 16 is a schematic curve showing the various features encountered. The initial stages of the impact (a) are characterized by a large displacement (relative to the total) but a low relative force. Next is a region (b) where the force rises fairly linearly with deformation.

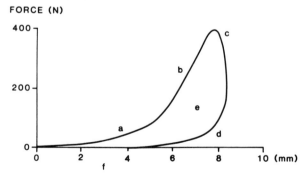

Figure 16 A typical hysteresis curve obtained from heel impact. See text for a detailed description of the various phases.

Following peak force (c), the displacement continues to increase slightly. This may be due to errors in the determination of the initial velocity which serves as an integration constant. The curve then exhibits a fall in both force and deformation (region d), but when the force reaches zero the deformation that still exists indicates that the original geometry of the heel has not been restored. Finally, the area marked (e) in Figure 16 represents the energy absorbed during impact measured in laboratory coordinates before being corrected for malleolus displacement (see below).

The rather distinctive "knee" in the rising phase of the force-deformation curve suggests that a suitable mechanical analog may be a linear spring with a stiffness that changes abruptly at a given deformation. Estimates of the two values for stiffness were made from six of the subjects under the standard impact conditions of 1.03 $m \cdot sec^{-1}$ and 1.9 kg. As shown in Table 2, the stiffness at the low deformations had a mean value of 0.19×10^5 $N \cdot m^{-1}$ (sd 0.05×10^5 $N \cdot m^{-1}$) while the average value at the higher deformation was almost one order of magnitude greater at 1.38×10^5 $N \cdot m^{-1}$ (sd 0.54×10^5 $N \cdot m^{-1}$). These values are between 5 and 10 times smaller than those quoted by Denoth and Nigg (1981).

The effect of increased velocity of impact upon the various parameters was also studied and the results are presented in Table 1. The peak force and the maximum deformation are higher, as may have been expected, and the energy absorbed is approximately 5% greater. It is clear

TABLE 2 Values for Initial Stiffness (IS) and Final Stiffness (FS) for Six Subjects During Impacts

Subject #	Condition 1 IS	FS	Condition 2 IS	FS	Condition 3 IS	FS
1	0.22	1.56	0.13	2.56	0.22	1.67
2	0.11	0.61	0.12	1.47	0.07	0.87
3	0.24	1.45	0.12	2.40	0.19	1.42
4	0.17	1.13	0.18	2.05	0.16	0.97
5	0.20	1.27	0.20	2.68	0.31	1.31
6	0.22	2.25	0.29	3.16	0.23	1.83
N = 6 Means	0.19	1.38	0.17	2.39	0.20	1.34

Condition 1: 1.90 kg mass, 1.03 $m \cdot s^{-1}$ velocity
Condition 2: 1.90 kg mass, 1.44 $m \cdot s^{-1}$ velocity
Condition 3: As for condition 1 but with 25 initial impacts before data collection.
All values in $N \cdot m^{-1} \cdot 10^5$

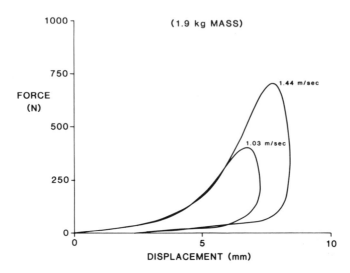

Figure 17   The effects of changing initial velocity on the heel impact hysteresis curve.

from Figure 17, however, that the rising phase of the force-deformation curves are virtually unaffected by the increased initial velocity up to the point where the lower velocity impact reaches peak force. Further combinations of mass and velocity to produce the same input energy are presented in Figure 18, and these results show that the rising phase of the force-deformation curves are again unaffected and, apart from minor

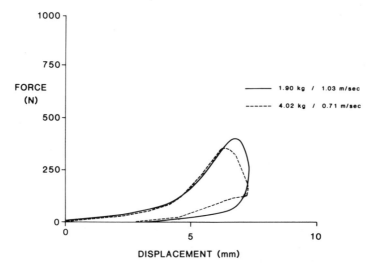

Figure 18   The effects of changing pendulum mass at the same input energy on the heel impact hysteresis curve.

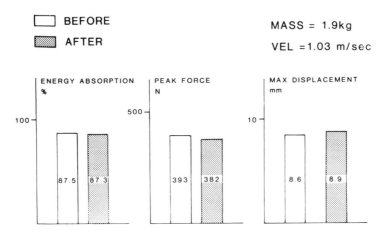

Figure 19   The effect of 25 repeated impacts on energy absorption, peak force, and maximum displacement.

anomalies, the curves are virtually identical throughout their course.

Figure 19 shows the effect of 25 successive impacts on the heel performed at a rate of about 1 every 3 seconds. The data indicates that the heel recovers rather quickly from each impact. When comparing the data from the 1st and 25th impacts, there are no significant differences between the energy absorption, peak force, or maximum penetration.

High-speed film was taken at 500 frames per second from the lateral side for a single subject at various initial impact velocities. This procedure enabled the impact velocity to be independently verified and allowed the motion of the whole lower leg during impact to be measured. Figure 20 shows the displacement of a marker on the lateral malleolus as a function of time for impacts at three different velocities. It is apparent that a maximum displacement of approximately 3 mm occurred in the 1.24 m·s^{-1} impact, and that the displacement peaks in this trial at approximately 15 ms after impact. When this measured displacement was subtracted from the deformation calculated in laboratory coordinates by double integration of the accelerometer curves, the basic shape of the hysteresis curves were unchanged, as shown in Figure 21. The corrected curve is shifted toward the origin, but because most of the malleolus displacement occurred before tissue deformation, such features as energy absorption remain unchanged by the correction.

A variety of mechanical or mathematical models could be used to produce a satisfactory simulation of the hysteresis curves shown in Figures 16 through 18. Figure 22 shows the results of applying the two-body collision model discussed by Misevich and Cavanagh (in press). The two colliding bodies are separated by a dashpot and a nonlinear spring, and the model allows the mass ratio of the bodies and the mechanical

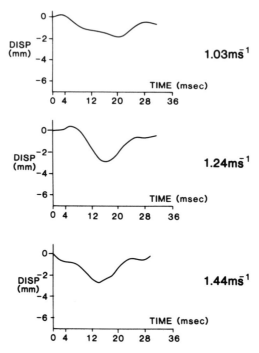

Figure 20 The displacement of a marker on the lateral malleolus during the impact of a single subject at three different initial velocities.

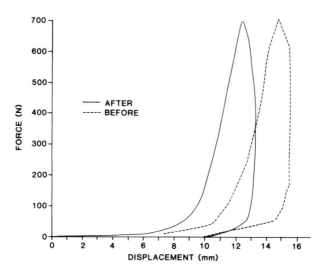

Figure 21 A heel impact hysteresis curve for a single subject corrected for the effect of malleolus displacement.

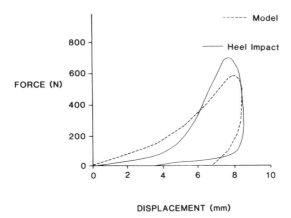

Figure 22   The output of the two body collision model compared to experimentally obtained data.

constants of the separating elements to be varied at will. The data in Figure 22 represent the output of one such run though the model where the motion of the impacting mass was considered at successive small time increments after an impact with an initial velocity of 1.41 m·s^{-1}.

The constants used in this particular run were:

Initial velocity: 1.41 m·s^{-1}
Spring constant: 0.25* 10^5 N·m^{-1}
Damping constant: 10 N (m·s^{-1})
Mass ratio: 2:1 (target: pendulum)
Time increment: 0.02 ms.

The fairly close agreement of the experimental and model curves indicate that the model chosen is a reasonable simulation of the actual impact phenomena observed during an impact with a mass of 1.9 kg at the same initial velocity.

IN-SHOE PRESSURE MEASUREMENTS

It is a relatively simple matter, as discussed earlier, to measure the net force components acting on the under-surface of the shoe during running. However, estimates of the contact area of the foot inside the shoe can be somewhat elusive and these would be needed for the calculation of average pressures at the shoe-foot interface. In light of the fairly rugged anatomical terrain on the plantar surface of the calcaneus, it is an open question as to whether these average pressures would be meaningful. A

Figure 23   An array of 64 piezoelectric pressure transducers encapsulated in a flexible substrate. This array was used to collect the pressure plots shown in Figure 24.

more direct approach to this problem is to measure the contact pressures using an in-shoe transducer array. A method for constructing and using such an array has been described in detail elsewhere (Hennig, Cavanagh, Macmillan, & Albert, in press).

Briefly, small piezoelectric ceramic tiles are embedded in a flexible substrate after suitable electrical connections have been made to their upper and lower surfaces. When vertical stresses are placed on the material, the resulting charge is amplified by an FET operational amplifier and the outputs from many such amplifiers are multiplexed to provide a single analog line, which is sampled by an AD converter. For the present study, the 64-element array shown in Figure 23 was constructed to fit inside the heel of a running shoe. The individual elements were 3mm × 3mm, and they were placed for the most part at center to center distances of 1 cm. In the rear part of the array, some elements were placed with a 5mm spacing.

Figure 24 shows a sequence of four diagrams collected from a single subject running at approximately 3 ms^{-1} on a treadmill. Each intersection of two lines in the display represents the location of a transducer, and the height of the display above the ground plane is proportional to the pressure at that location. The initial display from 39 ms after first contact shows pressure building in a fairly uniform manner over a 3 cm region along the posterior midline of the heel. There is some evidence that pressure is greatest at a point 2 cm forward of the most posterior elements and this is confirmed by the later displays for 44, 51, and 54 ms. A fairly abrupt drop in the pressure measured by the anterior 3 rows of transducer elements, and by the medial and lateral rows, is also evident at all times shown in Figure 24. Peak pressures be-

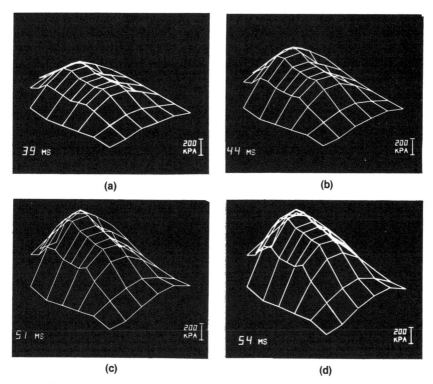

(a)   (b)

(c)   (d)

Figure 24   Plots of spatial distributions of pressure underneath the heel of a single subject running on the treadmill at 3 m·s^{-1}.

tween 0.5 and 1 MPa were recorded from the transducer and, following this peak loading, there was a dwell period when the pressure decayed only slightly before weight was finally transferred to other regions in the shoe. Further work with in-shoe transducers is continuing at Penn State University; it is also anticipated that pressure distribution measurements can be made during impact experiments of the kind described earlier in the section on heel properties to compare the in-shoe and experimental situations.

CONCLUDING REMARKS

This paper has attempted to give a biological perspective on the approaches needed in the formulation of a model of the shoe-foot interface. Any successful model must account for the observed kinematics and kinetics of the foot during running, and it must incorporate the material properties of the biological tissues as well as similar properties for the shoe materials. Variability is the hallmark of most biological phenomena, and modeling becomes even more rewarding in the presence of such variability because the effects of the parameter variation can be easily studied. It is hoped that this work will stimulate further developments that are greatly needed in this area of biomechanics.

ACKNOWLEDGMENTS

This work was supported in part by a research grant from Colgate-Palmolive/Etonic to The Pennsylvania State University in 1981. The contributions of Horst Albert, Mario Lafortune, and David Petrie are gratefully acknowledged.

REFERENCES

Batty Shaw, H.A. Contribution to the study of the morphology of adipose tissue. *J. Anat. and Physiol.* **36**:1-13, 1902.

Blechschmidt, E. Die Architektur des Fersenpolsters. *Morphol. Jahrb.* **72**:20-68, 1933. (Reprinted as: The structure of the calcaneal padding: Foot and ankle. 2(5):260-283, 1982.)

Cavanagh, P.R. *The running shoe book.* Anderson World, Mountain View, CA, 1980.

Cavanagh, P.R., and Lafortune, M.A. Ground reaction forces in distance running. *J. Biomechanics* **13**(5):397-406, 1980.

Day, M.H., and Napier, J.R. A hominid toe bone from bed 1, Olduvai Gorge, Tanzania. *Nature* **211**:929-930, 1966.

Denoth, J., and Nigg, B.M. The influence of various sport floors on the load on the lower extremities. In: A. Morecki, K. Fidelus, K. Kedzior, and A. Wit (eds.), *Biomechanics VII-B,* University Park Press, Baltimore, MD, 1981.

Hennig, E.M., Cavanagh, P.R., Macmillan, N.H., and Albert, H.A. The measurement of the vertical contact stresses on the plantar surface of the foot. *J. Biomech. Eng.,* in press.

Kuhns, J.G. Changes in elastic adipose tissue. *J. Bone and Joint Surg.* **31-A**:541-547, 1949.

Miller, W.E. The heel pad. *Am. J. Sports Med.* **10**(1):19-21, 1982.

Misevich, K.W., and Cavanagh, P.R. Material aspects of modeling shoe/foot interaction. In: E.C. Frederick (ed.), *Sport shoes and playing surfaces.* Human Kinetics, Champaign, IL, 1984.

Nigg, B.M., and Denoth, J. *Sportplatzbelage.* Juris Druck und Verlag, Zurich, 1980.

Steinbach, H.L., and Russell, W. Measurement of the heel-pad as an aid to diagnosis of acromegaly. *Radiology* **82**:418-423, 1964.

Wells, H.G. Adipose tissue—A neglected subject. *J. Am. Med. Assn.* **114**(22): 2177-2183, and **114**(23):2284-2289, 1940.

CHAPTER THREE

Material Aspects of Modeling Shoe/Foot Interaction

K.W. Misevich and P.R. Cavanagh

The basic problem in running shoes is impact — body to ground and heel to shoe. With the great surge in long distance running, the need to protect people has become paramount. Here, the materials aspect of the shoe as part of the shoe/foot system will be described in detail. This work is a broad stroke of screening tests that will provide a feeling for the basic interactions of the system components. System definition is the scope of the material aspects of modeling the shoe/foot interaction, and will largely be confined to the shoe. The characteristics of the heel are addressed in the companion paper on the biological aspects.

Running has already drawn attention from many disciplines, both academic and industrial. The shoe has enjoyed great scrutiny. Its history is fully chronicled in *The Running Shoe Book*. However, the biomechanical demands placed on shoe materials require that the analysis of the shoe/foot system have coordination and synergism of many points of view. This paper will present the flow of work in a joint Penn State/ Etonic project funded in April 1981 to develop an effective predictive model for the heel region in the shoe/foot interface.

Running shoes are effective in cushioning shock to the body, but there is some confusion in how and why they work. The various data that have given rise to many controversies need step by step consolidation into a unified picture. The system must be examined with concepts that can be modeled mathematically. Each parameter must be considered,

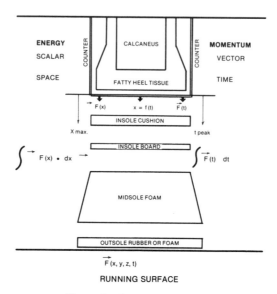

Figure 1   Shoe/foot system.

weighed, and utilized until we are certain that none of the major effects have been missed.

The system to be defined is shown schematically in Figure 1. Two very basic concepts are to be emphasized: energy and momentum—their conservation, their independence, and their practical interactions.

Momentum conservation must be reemphasized even though impulse measurements have dominated investigations up to this point. Equal and opposite forces are acting from the body, through the heel, through the shoe, and to the surface—all simultaneously. Unless considered as a system, there really is no single intuitive way to follow the momentum exchanges throughout the running heel impact or even in test situations.

Energy conservation is much more difficult because input from the body is at present indeterminant. Further, the elastic/inelastic absorptions partitioned among the components are significantly time and geometry dependent. Exhaustive searches through the literature have yielded little understanding of the components specifically as used in running shoes. This is especially true of the closed cell foams used as midsoles.

As we follow the path toward a proposed system model, each interaction relevant to the system function is considered in enough detail to create a general picture of its part of the whole running cycle. It is a subsystem with these limitations:

1. The model is one-dimensional, normal to the surface, with no consideration of shear forces nor angle of heel strike. However, transverse geometry enters with bearing surfaces and energy distributions.

2. No implications for the model will be drawn with respect to the interface with the body nor the running surface except as a boundary condition.

3. Several aspects of the model will be discussed in terms of typical results and introduced as mechanisms through inductive reasoning. The emphasis will be on trends in the agreement with experimental data.

4. Only the generic properties of component materials will be used for the sake of continuity.

GENERAL MATERIAL REACTIONS

It would be nice if elastic conditions would allow the use of the finite element method (FEM) to evaluate the stress distributions in the shoe. But this is for simple stable materials at very low strains; this condition just does not exist in running shoe materials. The combination of asymmetrical three-dimensional geometry and the time effects puts the problem right at the edge of computer stress analysis state of the art. The cost and complexity would be prohibitive.

The material system that we are investigating is determined by many actions imposed upon it. Previous action creates a material that is truly in a metastable state. The basic polymers, fibers, and resin matrices can vary widely in properties initially. Storage time, process conditions, and the myriad of intractables cause an unavoidable spread in the finished product. Embrittlement, degradation, and assembly variations all cause variations in the materials that are to be used or tested. Present action changes the material system each time it is imposed. The magnitude and duration are critical to the rate of permanent system changes which can mask the basic mechanisms. The higher the energy density, the more change possible. Thus, the geometrical distributions of forces and deformations can lead to erroneous conclusions in the interpretation of raw test data. Running shoes are very difficult to test even for simple impact.

Before looking at the shoe system in particular the principles of analysis—energy and momentum—should be examined more closely. Figure 2 depicts a general material system that is deformed by an external force. External energy is imposed as this force causes deformation. The system responds to a space change of state by increasing its internal energy, some into elastic recoverable potential energy and the rest lost by

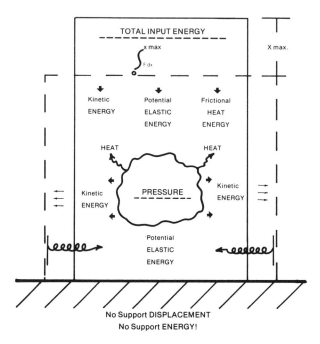

Figure 2   Space change of state.

a number of complicated mechanisms to heat. All of the energy applied to the system (the sum of all local pressures acting to cause incremental volume changes) is absorbed by the system—until the external action ends.

Consider a hypothetical space deformation of a material and follow the same force with time, as shown in Figure 3. Here we give the material a deformation in a fast step, but not so fast as to exceed the longitudinal velocity of sound in the medium and create shock waves. Whatever the force looks like plotted against space, the energy put into the system is the area under the curve up to the maximum deformation. This curve will generally increase in steepness with increasing rate of deformation. Looking at the same force with respect to time shows the reason. The faster the deformation, the less time there is for internal stress relaxation.

At peak deflection, the force still decays with time, but no energy is transferred out of the system mechanically. The system is responding to the causal input energy by changing state morphologically and thermally. After the action ends, potential energy continues to be lost by internal deformations—thus permanent set. As the deforming mechanism is removed, energy will be reclaimed, again its magnitude depending on the rate of withdrawal. The material is left stressed internally and will

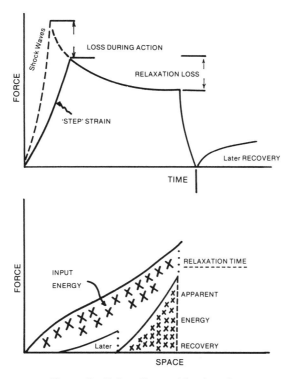

Figure 3   Relaxation and hysteresis.

therefore tend to move back toward its original state. Later, more energy is recoverable.

It is clear that a material system absorbs energy by providing a force that resists its deformation by an external cause, but whatever the contribution from the "molecular springs" in the material, part of the resisting force is inertial in nature. As shown in Figure 4, we see that a system responds to a time change of state in relation to the rate imposed by the external action. If we assume this external action is a free moving body, then associated with it is a scalar kinetic energy and a vector momentum. With a normal impact, there is momentum initially only in one dimension. The total one-dimensional momentum is constant and is dispersed in the system. The sum of all transverse momenta is zero!

While the total energy and momentum are conserved independently, they do interact in their distribution throughout the system. It is very difficult to understand this intuitively. The apparent stiffness, and thus the energy input per unit deformation, increases with impact velocity for two reasons: mass acceleration forces are added to the system response; and the elastic forces have less time to decay.

Accelerometers are commonly used to determine the forces acting

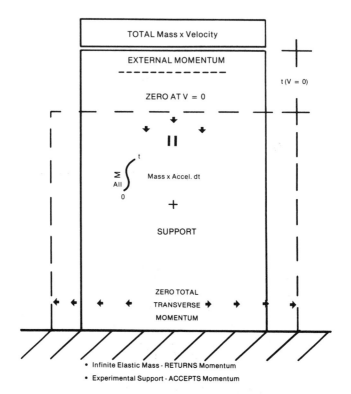

Figure 4 Time change of state.

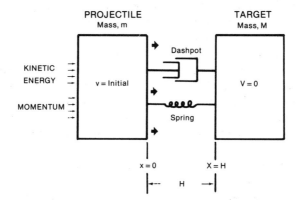

Dashpot Force = - Constant x|v-V|
Spring Force = f (H- (x-X))/f (x-X)
(Infinite Force at Touch)

Figure 5 Two body collision.

on a body during impact, but the data resulting from running shoe studies seem to vary much more than might be expected. Part of the problem is the difficulty in understanding or seeing the effects of the collision mechanics. For example, consider the one-dimensional impact of two bodies separated by a dashpot and a spring, as shown in Figure 5. The dashpot force is directly proportional to the relative velocity between the projectile and target. It provides a mechanism for converting energy to heat. The spring, on the other hand, is purely elastic but nonlinear simply for computational convenience. That is, a factor is added to provide an infinite force if the bodies touched, but it is of little consequence to this discussion.

The problem can easily be solved by numerical computer iteration. The flow chart is given in Figure 6. In a small time step, the forces are calculated and applied to both bodies. Incremental movement is determined from the relative velocities. It is a simple model which runs quickly. The force-time plots, even though a true simulation of accelerometer output, are straightforward. But if force is plotted against projectile position, as is common in shoe impacts, then some amazing results are seen!

Figure 6 is a family of curves for two masses and two energies with values relative to experiments made on the heel in the biological aspects of this study. Rebound and follow through, depending on mass ratios, should be expected. But the intuitive feeling fails with the dashpot present. The smaller mass has zero energy at its maximum movement in the laboratory coordinate system, not at its point of maximum force. If equal to the mass target, then the projectile still continues forward. With no dashpot, all of the energy would go through the spring to the target and would stop the projectile. Collision dynamics must be included in the interpretation, analysis, and testing of all impacts in the real world, where ideal infinite masses and pure elasticity do not exist.

STEP, dt	Small time increment
CALCULATE, v dt	Projectile position and gap
CALCULATE, F (x)	Spring and dashpot forces
CALCULATE, F/m dt & F/M dt	Both velocities
CALCULATE, V dt	New target position
CALCULATE	New kinetic energies
ADJUST FOR TRUE GAP	From latest positions
CALCULATE, F dx	Energy in spring
SUM, F dx	Energy lost in dashpot
CHECK, (x-X) > H?	Collision over?
STEP, dt	If not, continue

Figure 6   Two body calculations (see Figure 5).

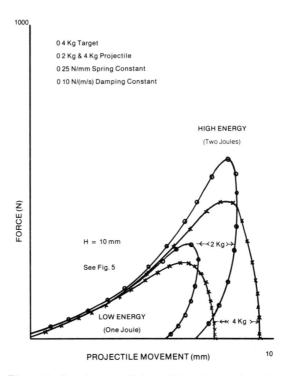

Figure 7   Two body collision, with spring and dashpot.

Since variation of the system components can yield any absolute output values, here are some of the trends observed:

- Increasing the target mass produces higher peak forces with less projectile travel. More energy is returned in the rebound; thus, the system appears to become more efficient. Equivalently, the coefficient of restitution goes up.
- Increasing the dashpot does not affect the projectile travel. The initial force is greater and the peak lower.
- Increasing the spring stiffness does reduce projectile travel but affects the peak force little. But remember, we have defined a special spring for this system.

In running, the masses are the body and the surface, but the body is segmented and both have distributed masses. Effective masses must be obtained from those who investigate the dynamics of the body and the surface as a system. They can then be entered as constraints to a shoe system model in the sense that they provide boundary inertial forces.

SIMULATED DROP TEST ON AN INSTROM

Predating the Sports Physics Lab at the Colgate-Palmolive Research Center, Etonic has funded research at the Penn State Biomechanics Lab in 1977 directed at the impact properties of running shoes.[1]

This included the drop test which created the proper impulse as observed with biomechanical force plate studies. The heel strike typically rises in force plates in about 20 milliseconds to 2.5 or more body weights (1800 N or about 400 lb) and occurs with a constant velocity something less than one meter/second. Dropping an 8.5 kg mass (18.7 lb) about 5 cm satisfies the conditions and allows rapid screening of running shoes and their constituent materials.

The Sports Physics Lab required test equipment more versatile than a dedicated drop test. This was to be the fastest light duty Instron Tester available in 1979.[2] The relevant characteristics of the model 1350 Instron are as follows:

- A 3000 psi source drives a servo-hydraulic ram from beneath. With an oversized valve, ram velocities of about 75 cm/sec are possible.

- The ram can be controlled in the stroke mode over its 5 in. (13 cm) range with a LVDT monitoring the position to better than 1%.

- The ram can also be controlled in the load mode to 2500 lb. (11 + kN) and is monitored by a precision DC strain gauge transducer mounted on the cross-head above.

- Besides the usual 10V control signals from a variable frequency function generator, the ram can be controlled in either mode by an external signal. This allows control and data acquisition by computer.

A Hewlett-Packard 9845A computer and 6940B multiprogrammer were interfaced to the Instron, providing 20K reading/sec for a single input and up to 450/sec for a simultaneous pair of inputs. Though slower, this was done to more easily monitor both stroke and load. While a 400-lb peak could be attained in 21 msec, less than 10 data pairs are received. To get better data and more of it, the rise time was slowed to about 45 msec. Remember that we are not near shock phenomena, as

[1]EPS/77.1 An Objective Evaluation of Training Shoes; EPS/77.2 A Summary Report of An Investigation of Forces under the Foot during Running; EPS/77.3 A Summary of Two Studies to Provide Quantitative Data on Track Shoes.

[2]Instron Corporation, 2500 Washington St., Canton, MA 02021.

noted in Figure 3. Separate tests show little change in the force hysteresis curves with this slowdown.

There are further basic differences between the drop test and the Instron:

- Maximum penetration is set by previous impacts to only approximate 400 lbs. minimum. But the rise portion of the curve was of most interest initially.
- The Instron has a 15-msec start-up to maximum velocity and then the velocity is constant for most of the impact.
- In most cases the total input energy *exceeded* the drop test energy.

Figure 8 shows, on one graph, typical computer curves of force/time, force/displacement, and displacement/time. Since peak accelerations were used most for comparisons, this was the first order of business. An equivalent "g" can be obtained from the Instron test by integrating the F-x hysteresis curve up to the point where the total drop test input energy is reached. If the force at this energy is normalized to the weight of the impacter, then the peak acceleration is determined.

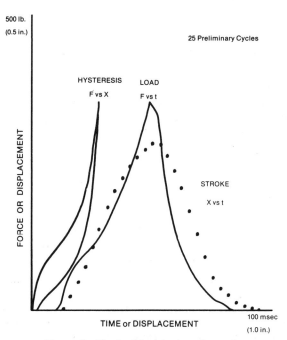

Figure 8 Typical fast Instron impact.

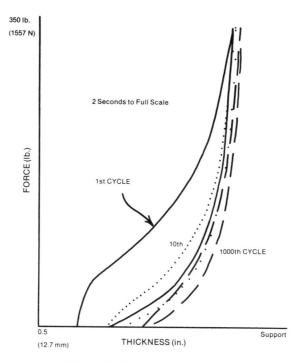

Figure 9   Typical cyclic impact.

Correlations were made on very many control and competitive shoes, with excellent results. There is confidence in screening prototypes and materials in this way, but with one important provision.

It soon became apparent that the impact results were very sensitive to cyclic impact history. This was recognized in the earliest Penn State tests by the requirement for 25 preliminary impacts before data acquisition. As the shoe is cycled, peak accelerations increase but at the same time the energy loss in the hysteresis decreases. The shoe becomes more efficient! Even slow (1 Hz) cycling shows this effect dramatically, as shown in Figure 9. The material takes a dynamic set and much higher forces are seen before the input energy is absorbed.

In order to evaluate the compression properties of a shoe with use, it was decided to sacrifice possible impulse rate effects and cycle the loading more slowly (1 Hz) while sampling continually. Figure 10 shows the typical result for the test as follows:

- Load is controlled to a 1Hz Haversine with a 400-lb peak.
- Load and stroke are sampled every 10 seconds for the first 100 cycles and thereafter uniformly on the logarithmic cycle scale.

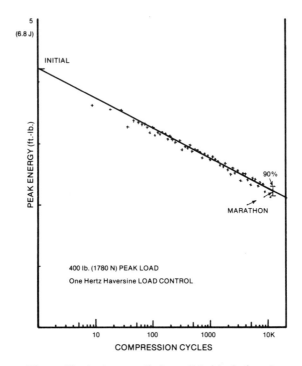

Figure 10   Instron cyclic impact (midsole foam).

- Between samplings the input energy is calculated and plotted. Also calculated and plotted are hysteresis loss, equivalent drop test g's, the penetration, and maximum thickness.

After 25 cycles, most shoes show a linear logarithmic decay in energy absorbed, partly due to a decreasing total thickness. As we shall see later, running shoes do restore themselves between uses!

Keeping with the broad stroke concept in this modeling process, it is better to study the system components separately to assess their relative importance to the whole impact process. Figure 11 shows the force-displacement on the return or rebound for just typical shoe components. The return is used because it more accurately reflects the elasticity — the return curve changes much more slowly with cyclic impact and is the return energy, in our case, to the body. All will certainly decay with continued cycling, but proportionally. These are all to the same maximum load so we can see roughly how the energy is partitioned in the shoe (see Figure 12).

For the modeling to continue, we must break down the shoe/foot system into its parts and find their elastic/inelastic mechanisms. The heel and its submodel are pursued separately in the biological aspects of this

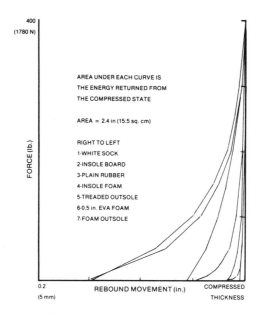

Figure 11   Typical shoe components (return force only).

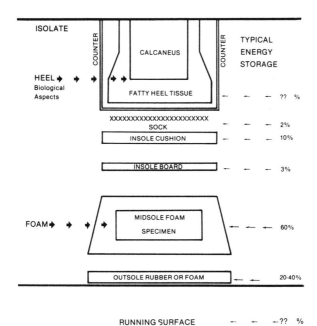

Figure 12   Shoe/foot system (energy partitions).

study. The shoe must first be viewed from its major energy and shock-absorbing component, the foam under whatever materials are in the shoe upper. Foam samples are therefore isolated conceptually and physically for testing. Correlations between the biological and material properties eventually provide a means of defining an interface condition to allow simultaneous solution of the mechanical dynamics. This means that equal and opposite forces at this interface be defined so as to be acceptable inputs to the submodels. In combination, they become the system model that can be used to predict total performance as geometry, materials, and external inputs are varied hypothetically.

DROP TEST SIMULATION AND PRELIMINARY FOAM MODEL

In order to correlate the hysteresis curves between the drop test and the Instron, we first performed representative drops on foam discs to establish penetration and peak loading for a definitive test sequence. A computerized test was then created to carefully copy the procedure as follows:

Samples of typical EVA running shoes are made up to the 1.75 in. (4.5 cm) diameter of the flat impacter utilizing a hole saw. The thickness is first automatically measured by slowly touching the surface to a load of about 1 lb. (0.5 Kg). Then to follow the drop test method, the sample is loaded to 18.7 lb. (8.5 Kg) to determine the baseline thickness with the drop weight on the sample. The total impact depth is then entered as the sum of the thickness difference and the previously observed drop penetration (about 7 cm). The sample is then impacted to this depth 25 times as in the drop test. The thicknesses are remeasured, the depth is entered, and a 10-second pause is introduced to mimic the typical restart drop test before the final impact with data collection is made.

Figure 13 shows the curves from each method on similar samples of EVA foam. The shapes of the rise are similar, but the peak is rounded in the drop and a large difference is seen in the hysteresis. The Instron rise time is about four times longer than the drop (45 msec vs. 12 msec) but this is only part of the discrepancy. Rate effects will be discussed in more detail later.

The details of the instrumentation and calculational methods of the drop test as compared with the Instron have many subtle nuances which are beyond the scope of this paper. However, we are convinced that the input energy and peak acceleration can be found equivalently by either method with little rate effect. The hysteresis requires much more attention.

Turning now to the preliminary foam model, consider the following facts and hypotheses: (a) Closed cell foams in running shoes are

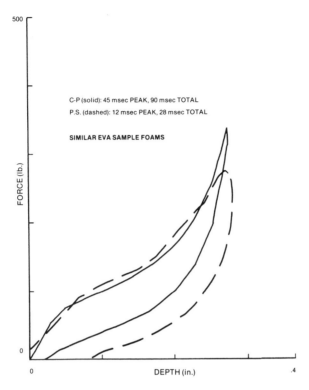

Figure 13   C-P/Penn State impact (Instron vs. drop hysteresis).

typically of a density of 0.2 gm/cc and are therefore about 80% gaseous. (b) From many careful Instron tests of typical foam samples, it is seen that the input energy absorption to the same peak load is directly proportional to thickness. The imaginary unit layers that make up the foam thicknesses are additive, just like ordinary spiral compression springs. (c) From scanning electron microscope photographs of many kinds of available foams, we see that the walls are very thin (less than 10 microns) and form their buckling creases with just a few impacts. The compressive column support forces can be neglected. (d) The foam typically used in running shoes can be considered as a pneumatic shock absorber. (e) Since the impact is a fast process, it will be assumed that each incremental deformation step compresses the gas adiabatically. Heat flow to the cell walls, however, must be included in the hysteresis energy loss. (f) Although there is something like 1/10th percent transverse expansion for every percent of compressive strain, it will be neglected for now. (g) Since the many running shoe foams tested do not bottom out to solid polymer under pressures in running, the gaseous volume is simply found from the foam and polymer densities. (h) Peak gas pressures do not exceed 10 atmospheres as a rule, so the gas can be considered as an ideal gas. Van der Waal effects enter slowly, anyhow. The mostly diatomic gas will have a specific heat ratio of 1.4.

The initial pneumatic foam model is easy to set up on the computer. Starting with the gas absolute pressure at one atmosphere, just a few inputs are required: the sample and impacter diameter, the thickness, the foam and polymer densities, the impacter weight and, finally, its initial drop height. The initial velocity and kinetic energy are calculated for the impacter just contacting the foam. The iteration procedure is simple:

- Start the space variable, X, at a foam thickness and increment.
- Calculate force from adiabatic pressure.
- Calculate new kinetic energy at the end of the step: previous plus the incremental gravitational potential energy minus the gas energy.
- Calculate velocity at end of step from kinetic energy.
- Calculate the incremental time lapse from the average velocity and keep summing for output marks every millisecond.
- Continue incrementing X until the impacter energy is absorbed.

A typical run is shown in Figure 14. The model as it stands cannot absorb enough energy to keep the peak accelerations down to the observed levels. At first, one might be tempted to say that we were too quick to neglect the contribution of the cell walls. But the nice thing about a computer model is that other "what ifs" can quickly be made. It turns out that a correlational can indeed be made if the gas is given a small additional internal pressure! Figure 15 shows the effect.

Experimental observations to justify this are: (a) Closed cell foams show a remarkable ability to quickly restore themselves nearly back to original dimensions after long cyclic testing, unlike open cell foams that must rely on the memory of the polymer. (b) Plunging a scalpel repeatedly into the foam while submerged in water shows a definite forced bubble release. (c) Compressing the foam to more than 10 atmospheres again while submerged shows negligible gas release. Only after several minutes do gas bubbles nucleate on the surface much like a carbonated drink. Clearly, the cell walls can withstand high pressures! (d) In foam manufacturing, blowing agents evolve gas while under very high clamping pressure. Calculation of final gas pressure for a known formulation and process with respect to initial and final dimensions indicates a residual pressure of something less than two atmospheres, absolute, if possible. This implies that cell walls are in tension!

A simple experiment proves this tension exists. If the gas in the foam were just at one atmosphere, then small positive and negative ex-

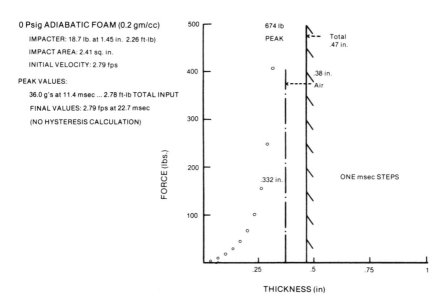

Figure 14   Drop test model.

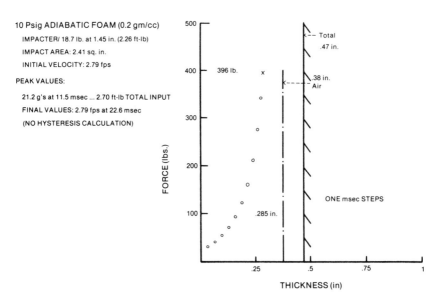

Figure 15   Drop test model.

cursions in the external pressure should yield about the same incremental changes in volume. A number of different foams were put into a vacuum chamber while the thickness was monitored continuously. Even though the internal pressure was effectively increased almost an atmosphere, none showed more than one-half percent expansion, far less than compression strains.

It is concluded, therefore, that running shoe foams do have some positive internal pressure that diffuses out only very slowly after manufacture. The pneumatic foam model is still viable for the observed impulse rises. But before expanding the model and introducing rate and hysteresis effects, the effective shape of the impacter must be considered. The human heel is clearly not a flat impacter. The triaxial pressure distribution must be considered. Here again, we have to turn to biomechanics.

GEOMETRY EFFECTS

As the body, leg, and heel first meet the surface we have to consider the hard rounded end of the calcaneus. However, it is covered with fatty tissue and fluid, which will change shape and move with the first contact. This must be studied separately until the basic mechanisms in the heel are known and understood. The pressure from the heel to the shoe insole will

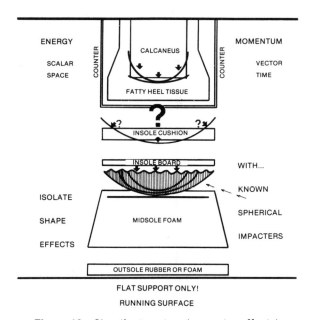

Figure 16   Shoe/foot system (geometry effects).

be affected by the constraint of the shoe counter, the stiffness of the insole components, and the rest of the system. Without assuming some boundary conditions, it is an indeterminant problem mechanically. So before even trying to consider the subtleties of the pressure distribution under the heel, we must view the system again as in Figure 16. There is no way yet to specify the shape of the impacter on the shoe or foam. It is a very difficult geometry which ultimately requires simultaneous solution.

So, again, the problem must be broken down into simpler parts. A basis must first be established in the foam, the major energy absorbing component, by examining its behavior with known pressure distributions.

In the study of clinical surfaces and mattresses, Small (1980) uses spherical impacters. He notes that the impacter penetration is related to the load per unit circumference. Similarly, we must see how the running shoe foam reacts to shaped impacters so as to be useful to the model. To this end, six spherical impacter heads with radii of 1/2, 3/4, 1, 2, 4, and 8 inches were substituted for the flat head impacter previously used.

Samples were cut from the same foam sheet (1.75 in. Dia., 0.5 in. thick) and impacted as previously described with a 45 msec rise time. The increasing force vs. depth curves are shown in Figure 17. (To avoid a clutter, the hysteresis is not included.) It is not surprising to see the apparent stiffness of the foam increasing with impacter radius; more

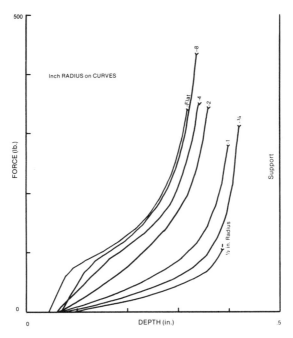

Figure 17 Spherical impacters (45 msec rise).

material is being compressed per unit penetration. If the force is divided by the projected circular area of the impacter in contact with the foam, not the surface of the spherical section, then we see a condensation of the family of curves into one basic shape as shown in Figure 18. The scatter is of the order of experimental variation.

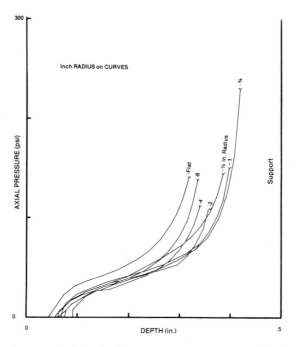

Figure 18   Spherical impacters (pressure normalized).

The important aspects of the shape of this family are the steep initial slope and the characteristic adiabatic gas compression curve that follows. Returning to the pneumatic model, it is reasonable to assume that a positive internal pressure must have a diffusion gradient to the foam surface. Therefore, a layer of cells with less than the average internal pressure must be engaged first. If the curves were extrapolated back to the original thickness, then the intercept would be an estimate of the internal pressure.

Although one would expect more transverse foam displacement with the smaller radii, the energy loss or hysteresis in this test sequence was in the range of 42 to 48% with no correlation to the radius. Later tests of shoes show only a small increase in loss as the radius goes down to one-half inch. The various aspects of hysteresis will be considered in the next section.

PROPOSED FOAM MODEL WITH HYSTERESIS

Now the complete foam impact process can be reviewed from start to finish so that the major elements of the proposed submodel can be drawn together. Start with the foam itself, a closed cell polymeric system with some cross-linking to make it more thermoset than thermoplastic. It is characterized by the cell size, wall thickness, and internal cell pressure. As previously discussed, the internal pressure will put the cell walls into a tension state. This tension, during fabrication, will tend to orient the polymers in the cells. The internal gas pressure restores the foam to a tension state even after long cyclic loading. Furthermore, there must be some pressure gradient to the surface because of diffusion.

An impacter must pass through a pressure gradient at the foam surface until the internal pressure is reached. At this point both the gas pressure and cell walls produce a force. The walls, however, will only contribute to the total stiffness for a limited number of cycles until preferred creases or hinges are formed. Even open celled foams with much heavier lattices and intersections absorb less than 10% of the energy of a closed cell foam. The wall contribution can safely be neglected.

The basic mechanism in closed-cell running shoe foams is gas compression. Since an impact cycle containing about 3 ft-lb (4 J) will only raise the temperature of the foam walls a part of a degree, the compression might be treated as an isothermal process. This is not true. In order for heat to be transferred at all to the polymer, the gas temperature must be higher. Then an incremental compression step must heat the gas adiabatically with transfer afterward. The understanding of heat transfer between a gas and a solid, and vice versa, is a very complex problem. This is especially true when the gas is confined in a space of the same order or less than its mean free path. Certainly the heat transfer coefficients, in and out of the solid, will not be equal. The gas has a mobility to give up kinetic energy much greater than the solid.

A gas compressed to around 10 atmospheres will increase in temperature several hundred degrees. Heat must be transferred, even in the fast pressure rise. Now if mechanical energy is lost as heat, according to Carnot cycle efficiency only a portion will be returned. The cycle's efficiency depends on the difference of absolute temperature in the system. Whatever the heat transfer rate, we can assume that most of the energy given by the gas to the polymer will be lost.

To see how much energy is involved, consider a volume of an ideal gas as it is compressed isothermally (constant temperature) and adiabatically (no heat transfer). Starting from some initial absolute pressure, both processes show pressure increase with the adiabatic being greater. If

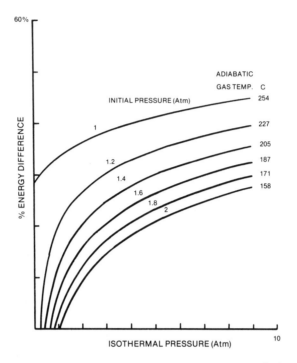

Figure 19   Adiabatic/isothermal (gas compression).

we calculate the energy input during the compression for each, then the total heat energy loss is just the difference between them.

Figure 19 shows a family of curves of the percent difference with respect to the adiabatic energy plotted against the isothermal final pressure in units of atmospheres. The greatest difference, and thus loss, occurs when the initial internal pressure is at one atmosphere. The family is formed by increasing the starting pressure 100% in 20% steps to two atmospheres, absolute. (Also shown are the adiabatic gas temperatures.) The faster the compression rate, the higher the temperature will rise, but only a heat transfer analysis will tell how high.

Running shoe foams see pressures in the range plotted. We would therefore expect to see hysteresis losses of approximately 30 to 50% of the input energy. This is the range of all the Instron impact data for all types of foams and shoes. But suppose the heat transfer is very fast compared to the compression rate, and the internal pressure is a good part of one atmosphere gauge. Then we could account for only 20 to 40% loss. What other mechanisms are possible?

Inasmuch as the cell walls could provide column forces, some frictional interaction might also be possible. This had to be very small in the impact direction. On the other hand, frictional shear in the transverse direction only acts to constrain the foam and is seen in the force curve through the gas pressure. All of this friction energy will be lost to heat, but it is still assumed to be a negligible part of the total input.

One would at first think that the tensile modulus of a foam would be very low. Indeed it will if tested normally. But suppose the foam were clamped flat and then stretched. Then the polymer would be oriented in the tensile direction and approach the modulus of a solid polymer sample. It could, under compression, become stiffer than the rubber outsole and even the insole board. Since the foam does expand transversely, there is clearly a mechanism for some additional loss. However, geometry again complicates this effect and requires much research.

In summary, it is concluded that the basic mechanism in closed cell foam is heat loss from the gas, so the frictional and tensile energies should be neglected in the first order model. But there are drop test results reported on foams and shoes that indicate greater losses than 50%. Why?

There are three explanations: (a) the transverse material dynamics, (b) instrumentation anomalies, and (c) analysis. The first is a real mechanism that can effectively prevent the return of energy to the impacter during the rebound phase.

As the cell walls heat up during compression, the surfaces where mechanical bending stiffness resides will be close to the gas temperature. Conversely, the outer surface will be frozen by the adiabatic cooling during the rebound. This means that on this fast time scale there will be a delay in contraction. The foam right under the impacter therefore will not see a pressure as great as if the process were slower.

Friction, of course, is always opposite the direction of motion and adds to the effect. The radial kinetic energy of the foam, though insignificant when compared to the impact energy, requires inertial forces for reversal. All the foam is initially under the flat impacter during compression, but a ring with an area of about 10% of the total is forced outward. It cannot provide return force. (Going from a lubricated to a bonded interface does show this effect.)

If the impacter is spherical, then additional radial velocity and energy is imparted. Still again, this is a small effect if one recalls the spherical impacter results.

It is thought that the transverse motion effects cannot account, in the extreme, for more than a few percentage points of the total loss. The latter two explanations can, on the other hand, produce large apparent losses. From the work in the biological aspects with drop and pendulum tests, it was found that calculating the shape of the force-space hysteresis curve is extremely sensitive to the value of the initial velocity. It involves a double integration from the accelerometer output. Since the Instron simultaneously measures force and position, no such problem exists.

Last, the two body collision example showed a definite distortion of the hysteresis in the laboratory coordinate system. Even small movements or deflections of the apparatus will contribute. It is up to the individual investigators to determine the magnitude of these effects in their equipment and account for it in the final output data.

The foam submodel has been taken as far as it can at this time. The utilization of these concepts lies in the computer iteration techniques of the drop model already discussed. At each step in space, heat loss, material and frictional forces can be added to the desired detail. All are then added into the total energy which is extracted from the impacter. As long as one remembers to apply equal and opposite forces to all movable effective masses, then momentum conservation will take care of itself. The iteration step size need only be small enough to achieve the precision desired in the summation of total energy and momentum.

SYSTEM SUMMARY

During the running gait the body as a whole will have cyclic vertical kinetic energy and momentum whose magnitudes can vary widely depending on the muscle interaction and the body linkage geometry. The body can change these according to the shoe surface to prevent excessive shock. But is harmful "shock" the impulse, the peak force, or the rate of change of force, called jerk? Biomechanics must define this and also define the total runner/surface dynamics and kinematics. However, in the final analysis, it is the detailed pressure distribution in the shoe/foot system that will normally determine the shape of the impulse. The travel, and thus time, over which the impact occurs will establish the peak force seen by the body. Remember that both the kinetic energy and momentum will by definition be zero simultaneously when the velocity is zero.

Consider the shoe/foot system as shown in Figure 20, and how the elements of the model are combined. The submodel for the heel developed in the biological aspects uses an ideal flat surface to deform the tissue. As the heel is constrained from transverse expansion, the inertial and viscoelastic contribution of the tissue increases, and the pressure distribution spreads out.

The first step in combining the heel model to the shoe is to define a manageable pressure distribution as a function of heel deformation. Ideally, a rigid calcaneus shape covered with an elastometric material would account for a major portion of the load observed experimentally. It is very important to keep the geometry simple even at the expense of accuracy because an experimental impacter is essential to the final system solution. It is also essential to proper evaluation of shoe designs.

Unless much time and money are spent on a full-blown 3D Finite

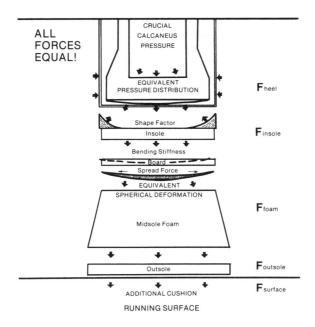

Figure 20   Shoe/foot system (final model).

Element analysis to develop analytical equations empirically, we cannot hope for a simultaneous solution for the elements of the system from first principles. The geometry is just too complicated. As we move down through the shoe we can see why. The insole material adds a little cushioning which can be handled easily in a one-dimensional model, but its interaction with the counter in shaping the heel tissue is intractable. It is felt that the crucial pressure to both the body and the shoe is that right under the calcaneus. It accounts for most of the energy and momentum transfer. An equivalent symmetrical pressure distribution must be used as input to the shoe. This distribution applied to the insole board, however thin, will determine the deformation of the foam. This deformation can be approximated by a spherical radius and applied to the foam submodel.

In order to solve the whole system, we must have empirical functions or data tables which provide force for a known displacement, or vice versa, for each element: heel tissue, insole, foam, outsole, and surface. In computer modeling it is common to search tables of experimental data even during the iteration procedure. At time zero, the force is zero and an initial kinetic energy assumed. We must also assume effective masses for the body and the surface, or else the dynamics and impulse are not obtainable, only a force/travel hysteresis.

To start, we increment the calcaneus displacement and keep looping through the elements until all forces are equal. That is, we have to partition the displacement and thus the energy. This force is then applied to both masses to determine the change in momentum and energy. Other than the simultaneous solution for the force in the elements, the problem is exactly the same as the two body collision illustration.

Computer modeling a system in this manner is completely general and can be updated as the force/displacement functions or experimental data are improved. Clearly, the more detail that is included in each element, the more internal loops will be required to satisfy proposed interaction between them, mechanically. An example would be the shear constraints at element interfaces. It should be apparent by now that the shoe/foot system cannot stand alone and be solved. While a general surface might be hypothesized for some type of running and maintained throughout screening runs, it seems that an inertial mass model for the body must be added as the input to the calcaneus.

Even though much work lies ahead, the manipulation of a computer model in even the rough form developed so far can have rich rewards. Variations in the parameters of each element submodel often effectively show up the basic phenomena and lead to new ideas in testing and design. It is the model, its creation, use, and interpretation that are most valuable. By being faithful to basic energy and momentum conservation, we are forced to uncover the primary mechanisms or else be doomed to failure in correlation and prediction.

ACKNOWLEDGMENTS

This joint project between Penn State and Colgate-Palmolive/Etonic has been very productive. Each of the many sessions with Gordon Valiant, Mario LaFortune, and Horst Albert generated new angles of perspective for the model and methods for testing them.

This work was possible through Dr. Henry Cross III at Colgate, whose commitment to the value of basic research in sports shoes provided the initial and continuing impetus. Likewise, the myriad of tests carefully conducted by John Puckhaber produced most of the data which allowed typical condensations to be made with certainty in this work. Finally, Liza McCoy expeditiously got the final manuscript in just under the wire.

REFERENCES

Foam Related

Baumann, H. Compression set—A doubtful criterion for assessing closed-cell flexible foams. *Kunstst. Ger. Plast.* **67**:11, 1977.

Bonner, W.H., et al. Pneumacel: Basic technology and applications. *J. Appl. Polymer Sci.* **24**:89-103, 1979.

Clarke, T.E., and Frederick, E.C. Dynamic load displacement characteristics of athletic shoe midsole materials. *Am. Soc. Biomechanics Meeting*, Cleveland, 1981.

Deanin, R.D., et al. Structure and properties of flexible vinyl foams. *Polymer Eng. Sci.* **14**:193-210, 1974.

Liber, T., et al. Shock isolation elements testing for high input loadings. USAF Space and Missile Systems Organization (SAMSO TR 69-118), NTIS No. AD-857686, 1969.

Meinecke, E.A., Schwaber, D.M., and Chiang, R. Impact analysis for cellular polymeric materials. *J. Elastoplast.* **3**:19-27, 1971.

Meinecke, E.A., and Schwaber, D.M. Energy absorption in polymeric foams. (I) Prediction of impact behavior from Instron data for foams with rate-independent modulus. *J. Appl. Polymer Sci.* **14**:2239-2248, 1970.

Moore, T.L. Voraspring support polymer — A new foam concept. *SPI Cell Plast. Div.,* Int. Cell Plast. Conf., Montreal, Technomic Publ., 1978.

Progelhof, R.C., and Throne, J.L. Young's modulus of uniform density thermoplastic foam. *Polymer Eng. Sci.* **19**:498-499, 1979.

Schwaber, D.M. Impact behavior of polymeric foams: A review. *Polymer-Plast. Technol. Eng.* **2**:231-249, 1973.

Small, C.F. Mechanical compliance evaluation of clinical support surfaces. *J. Biomechanics* **13**:315-322, 1980.

Wasley, R.J., et al. *Techniques for studies of low-stress dynamic mechanical behavior of materials: Results for foam like materials.* Lawrence Livermore Lab, U. Calif., UCID-16135.

Biomechanics

Alexander, R. McN., and Jayes, A.S. Fourier analysis of forces exerted in walking and running. *J. Biomechanics* **13**:383-390, 1980.

Cavanagh, P.R., and Michiyoshi, A. A technique for the display of pressure beneath the foot. *J. Biomechanics* **13**:69-75, 1980.

Dainis, A. Whole body and segment center of mass determination from kinematic data. *J. Biomechanics* **13**:647-651, 1980.

Draganichi, L.R., et al. Electronic measurement of instantaneous foot-floor contact patterns during gait. *J. Biomechanics* **13**:875-880, 1980.

Haberl, R., and Prokop, L. Physiological aspects of synthetic tracks. *Biotelemetry* **6**:171-178, 1974.

Hawes, D., et al. Modeling the distortion produced by heel strike transients in soft tissue. *Proc. Physiological Soc.* pp. 10-11, 1979.

Larsen, R.D. The kinetics of running. *J. Chemical Education* **56**:651-652, 1979.

Lees, S. A model for bone hardness. *J. Biomechanics* **14**:561-567, 1981.

Light, L.H., McLellan, G.E., and Klenerman, L. Skeletal-transients on heel strike in normal walking with different footwear. *J. Biomechanics* **13**:477-480, 1980.

Lord, M. Foot pressure measurement: A review of methodology. *J. Biomed. Eng.* **3**:91-99, 1981.

Mann, R.A., Hagy, J.L., and Simon, S.R. *Biomechanics of gait: A critical visual analysis.* Gait Analysis Lab, Shriners' Hospital for Crippled Children, San Francisco, 1975.

McConville, J.T., et al. *Anthropometric relationships of body and body segment moments of inertia.* USAF Aerospace Medical Research Lab, Wright-Patterson AFB, OH (AFAMRL-TR-80-119), 1980.

McMahon, R.A., and Greene, P.R. The influence of tract compliance on running. *J. Biomechanics* **12**:893-904, 1979.

Onyshko, S., and Winter, D.A. A mathematical model for the dynamics of human locomotion. *J. Biomechanics* **13**:361-368, 1980.

Robertson, D.G.E., and Winter, D.A. Mechanical energy generation, absorption and transfer amongst segments during walking. *J. Biomechanics* **13**: 845-854, 1980.

Scranton, P.E. Jr., and McMaster, J.H. Momentary distribution of forces under the foot. *J. Biomechanics* **9**:45-48, 1976.

Van Ingen Schenau, G.J. Some fundamental aspects of the biomechanics of overground versus treadmill locomotion. *Med. & Sci. in Sports and Exercise* **12**: 257-261, 1980.

Model Related

Cavanagh, P.R. *The running shoe book.* Anderson World, Mountain View, CA, 1980.

Conway, H.D., et al. Force-time investigations for the elastic impact between a rigid sphere and a thin layer. *Int. J. Mech. Sci.* **14**:523-529, 1972.

Conway, H.D., et al. The impact between a rigid sphere and a thin layer. Trans. ASME, *J. Appl. Mechanics*, March 1970.

Dauer, R.W. Experimental determination of impact force vs. displacement curves. *Experimental Mechanics*, pp. 159-160, April 1978.

Engel, P.A., and Lasky, R.C. Mechanical response and heat buildup in repetitively impacted elastomers. *Experimental Mechanics*, pp. 99-105, March 1977.

Fisher, H.D. The impact of an elastic sphere on a thin elastic plate supported by a Winkler foundation. Trans. ASME, *J. Appl. Mechanics*, March 1975.

Gilman, J.J. Relationship between impact yield stress and indentation hardness. *J. Appl. Phys.* **46**, April 1975.

Hutchings, I.M. Energy absorbed by elastic waves during plastic impact. *J. Phys. D: Appl. Phys.* **12**, 1979.

Johnson, G.R. Analysis of elastic-plastic impact involving severe distortion. Trans. ASME, *J. Appl. Mechanics*, pp. 439-444, Sept. 1976.

Phillips, J.W., and Valvit, H.H. Impact of a rigid sphere on a viscoelastic plate. Trans. ASME, *J. Appl. Mechanics*, pp. 873-878, Dec. 1967.

Prigogine, I. Thermodynamics of irreversible processes. *American Lecture Series #185.* Chas. Thomas Publ., Springfield, IL, 1955.

Sobel, M.I. Kinetic derivation of the adiabatic law for ideal gases. *Am. J. Phys.* **48**:877-878, Oct. 1980.

Tsai, Y.M., and Dilmanian, K. Impact of spheres on elastic plates of finite thickness. *Devel. in Mechanics* **6**:1009-1022, 1970.

Materials Theory

Barkan, P. Impact. *Mechanical design and systems handbook* (H.A. Rothbart, ed.). McGraw-Hill, New York, 1962.

Gordon, P., et al. The influence of dynamic yield point in multimaterial impact. *J. Appl. Physics* **8**:172-179, Jan. 1977.

Meinecke, E.A. *Comparing the time and rate dependent mechanical properties of elastomers.* ACS Rubber Div. 117th Meeting, Las Vegas, May 1980.

Schmidt, A.X., and Marlies, C.A. Rheology. *Principles of high polymer theory and practice.* McGraw-Hill, New York, 1948.

Sharma, M.G. Dynamic behavior of rubber. *The vibration and acoustic measurement handbook* (M.P. Blake and W.S. Mitchell, eds.). Spartan Books, 1972.

Ungar, E.E. Mechanical vibrations. *Mechanical design and systems handbook* (H.A. Rothbart, ed.). McGraw-Hill, New York, 1962.

Wu, L.M., Meinecke, W.A., and Tsai, B.C. *Prediction of creep behavior from stress relaxation data for nonlinearly viscoelastic materials.* ACS Rubber Div. Meeting, Cleveland, Oct. 1977.

Materials Testing

American Society for Testing and Materials. *Physical testing of plastics.* ASTM Special Technical Publication STP 736, 1981.

Bassi, A.C. Dynamic modulus of rubber by impact and rebound method. *Polymer Eng. Sci.* **18**:750-754, 1978.

Busche, M.G. Special report — Mechanical properties and tests — A to Z. *Materials Engineering*, June 1967.

Hillberry, B.M. (ed.) *The measurement of the dynamic properties of elastomers and elastomeric mounts.* Soc. Automotive Engineers, Inc., 1973.

Hunt, K.H., and Crossley, F.R.E. Coefficient of restitution interpreted as damping in vibroimpact. Trans. ASME: *J. Appl. Mechanics*, pp. 440-445, June 1975.

Skeletal Heel Strike Transients, Measurement, Implications, and Modification by Footwear

Gordon E. MacLellan

Heel strike is generally referred to as the first instant of contact between the heel and the floor in gait analysis. Thus it is instantaneous and as small as the powers of resolution of the recording equipment. However, here I would like to expand that definition to include the first 20 milliseconds of gait, this being a time period where, by modifying footwear construction, I shall demonstrate it is possible to engineer transients generated in the skeleton — thereby influencing the generation of musculoskeletal injuries and their response pattern. Furthermore, I would like people to think of what happens in the body as the result of heel strike transients in three-dimensional terms.

MEASUREMENT OF HEEL STRIKE TRANSIENTS

Earliest measurements of heel strike transients were via force platforms mounted on the floor. However, these do not represent what is actually happening within the skeleton at different levels since all the tissue layers in the skeleton have their own capacity for energy absorption. For example, when jumping up and down on one leg the adult femur bows and reduces its overall height by as much as one centimeter. Articular cartilage is known to be visco-elastic in many of its physical properties, but

TABLE 1   Skeletal Shock Forces— Attenuation in the Body

Active	*Passive*
Proprioception	Elasticity of bone
Joint position	Elasticity of cartilage
Muscle tone	Elasticity of soft tissues
	heel pad
	intervertebral discs
	? menisci

its capacity to absorb energy is different in different planes. Third, the soft tissues both beneath the heel and within the intervertebral disc structure have substantial energy absorbing capability, as has been shown in laboratory experiments. Thus, to evaluate the magnitude of forces that are actually generated within the skeleton, invasive technology had to be developed in order to get a true recording within the bone of the shock wave passing through the skeleton.

Previous experiments had been conducted using skin mounted accelerometers and this is clearly a suitable method for comparison of different footwear materials within the same individual. However, bonding techniques must be carefully controlled and accelerometers must always be mounted in exactly the same place. Furthermore, with the advance of time and the change with age of the physical properties of the collagen in the deeper layers of the skin, errors are bound to arise.

In order to get some standardization of the relationship between the transients on the skin and those in bone, as well as the transients at head level compared with at shin level, an experiment was devised whereby a lightweight accelerometer of extended frequency response was coupled to the tibia by a rigid system with Kirschner wires. A second accelerometer was bonded to a metallic bite bar held in the mouth between the teeth, and a third was bonded to a spreader plate that was fastened to the shin with adhesive and then further secured with elastic strapping. These three techniques of coupling were regarded as the most efficient way to eliminate errors.

By this technique, it was possible to compare the magnitude of the heel strike transients at each point as well as the pattern in which they arose. Furthermore, by comparing barefoot walking with different heel constructions, it was possible to clearly identify the difference between types of footwear. Subsequent clinical research has led us to believe that these differences are clinically significant.

The best transients available for interpretation are those demonstrated in the tibia. On barefoot walking at heel strike there is a rapid deceleration of the tibia, reaching a peak of approximately 7G. The slope

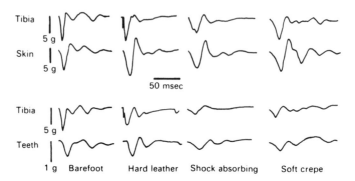

Figure 1 Waveform and order of magnitude of longitudinal acceleration transient on heel strike in normal walking on a hard floor with different footwear. Top pair: simultaneous tracings from tibia/shin surface transducers. Bottom pair: simultaneous tracings from tibia/bitebar transducers. From Light, MacLellan, and Klenerman (1979).

of the curve is very steep and there is a small recoil phenomenon. The wave's shape on the skin is somewhat similar, although the peak is slightly broader and the maximum peak slightly lower. At head level the tooth-mounted accelerometer revealed a peak just less than 1G with a slightly flatter slope. The values for a hard leather heel construction were somewhat similar, but a soft crepe rubber-soled shoe with a heel height of 18 millimeters demonstrated that although the peak transient was reduced to between 2.5 and 4G with a flatter slope there was rather marked reverberation within the bone of the tibia, although some of this had been damped by the time it reached the head.

The most impressive result, however, was achieved by using a modified polyurethane with high hysteresis as an insert in the posterior one-third of the heel. This was 6 millimeters thick and, mounted in an otherwise hard heel construction, produced a slightly greater reduction in heel strike transients than 18 millimeters of soft crepe rubber. Furthermore, the reverberation phenomena seen with a crepe rubber construction were not seen with this material, a polyurethane specifically engineered to avoid recoil while still under load.

MEDICAL EFFECTS OF HEEL STRIKE SHOCK WAVES IN RESEARCH

The observation that heel strike transients within the skeleton can be modified substantially through shock-absorbing heel construction has ushered in a new field of research, both in the management and origins of degenerative musculoskeletal conditions. In 1953, Lloyd-Roberts et al. demonstrated the effect of mechanical impact upon the articular cartilage of the rabbit knee and established a clear time relationship between mechanical insult, detritus formation within the joint, synovitis, and subsequent joint destruction.

Serink, Nachemson et al. in 1977 repeated this work with a carefully controlled impact load upon the rabbit knee, using the opposite knee as a control. All the knees pounded in this way produced the biochemical and histological changes of osteoarthrosis in a very short time. Radin et al. repeated this study and, having confirmed Nachemson's findings, performed an experiment with sheep in which two groups of sheep were kept under identical conditions except that some lived their lives on soft ground and others on concrete. They were all exercised for similar periods of time at about the same time every day. At 6 months of age, the sheep on the concrete surfaces were developing the biomechanical and histological changes of osteoarthrosis in their knee joint cartilage.

With the passage of time, however, there was some remodeling of the bony structure of the joint and some of the acute inflammatory changes regressed. This experiment was continued until the sheep were some 2 years of age. It therefore showed that in the sheep it is possible for the skeleton to modify itself in response to the shock forces placed upon it. Had the sheep been followed to old age, it would have been interesting to see whether the two groups subsequently developed typical osteoarthrosis.

EFFECTS OF SHOCK FORCES IN SPORTS

Observations in man have clearly demonstrated over the years the relationship between shock waves and arthritis. Where sport is concerned, everyone in the sports medicine field is familiar with the early degeneration in jumpers' knees, particularly those engaged in triple jump. Estimates of the heel strike deceleration in triple jumpers have been put as high as 30G. In my own experiments in 1977, we attempted to get an accurate recording of running heel strike transients but these were so high that the resonant frequency of the recording system was exceeded and we were not able to get a peak reading. However, this fact alone illustrates that when running on a hard surface in bare feet, heel strike transients between 10 and 15G are generated regularly.

It is common observation that different athletes heel strike with a different magnitude of force. Sitting beside an indoor running circuit on boards such as that at Harvard University and listening to the sounds of heel strike produced by different runners, one can clearly detect different forces generated even by individuals of the same size running at the same speed. This is only to be expected, considering the variability of the pattern of foot strike during running between heel strikers and mid-foot strikers; and force platform recordings clearly illustrate that there is a scatter of normals. We how have a duty to identify the athletes at risk and protect them as much as possible.

We are all familiar with the clinical phenomena that result from athletic pursuit on hard surfaces. Classic among these is Achilles tendinitis, but equally common is the troublesome subcalcaneal pain experienced particularly by young athletes — torn calf muscles, hamstring tears, and low backache. Many of these are particularly aggravated on some synthetic turf surfaces that have little natural energy absorption. In Britain we have problems with our cricketers who train and play on relatively soft grass during the English cricket season and then travel overseas to compete on hard and unyielding surfaces, with a high injury rate as a consequence.

Where the grounds are very hard, shin soreness, backache, and heel pain are so common as to be regarded as normal. Our professional football players train in the spring and early winter on grass, but are frequently confined indoors during bad weather. During this time they have a high incidence of Achilles tendon problems and heel pain. One of the clubs we studied noted an alarmingly high incidence of low backache on synthetic turf in their indoor training facility.

The relationship between sport and osteoarthritis has long been established, particularly in the hip joint. It is well known that following meniscectomy in the knee for top-level athletes, early degenerative articular disease is almost the rule. This is particularly so when there has been ligament injury. But even in its absence there is substantial evidence of early osteoarthritis. In short, there is extensive evidence that shock absorption in sporting footwear must play a part both in the prevention of long-term degenerative joint disease and short-term soft tissue failures.

The immediate significance of the relationship between hard heel strike and soft tissue distortion is well illustrated by high-speed cine film. As the heel hits the ground, a ripple is seen to flow proximally from the heel indicating the horizontal transmission of the shock wave from the bone to the soft tissue. On modeling this distortion, it is clear that while the hard core is displaced the soft tissue is left behind, briefly generating at the interface traction and shear phenomena. We now believe it is this shear phenomenon operating in the tissues that give support to the very tenuous and fragile blood supply of the Achilles tendon that results in the chronic hypoxic changes demonstrated on histochemistry of the Achilles tendon in Achilles tendinitis.

There is now extensive clinical experience of shock absorption in footwear wherein Achilles tendinitis is partially or completely resolved by the reduction of the heel strike transient by inserts made of Sorbothane. In the past, similar benefit has been observed by using plastazote and orthopedic felt, but it is clear that this effect is only achieved after large volumes of inserts have been used. Using the high polymer technology of Sorbothane, it is possible to achieve the same degree of shock absorption with a minimal heel raise and, as a result, apply the shock absorption to conventional sports footwear with great confidence. While in recent years this has been achieved by inserts either exclusively in the heel section of the shoe or as a complete insole, the emergence of the market of sports shoes specifically designed to have energy absorption in the heel and beneath the ball of the foot suggests a major breakthrough in foot comfort in running as well as in the prevention of soft tissue injuries.

The use of this type of material has paved the way for developing a low profile sports shoe that can be slimmer and lighter than conventional high energy-absorbing training shoes, and have the added advantage of stability on uneven surfaces. Since the heel of the shoe does not have to be unduly raised, the tendency of tightening the calf muscle, induced by some types of running shoe, can hopefully be avoided. This is not to say that runners should not begin their activities with a program of stretching the calf and hamstring muscles in order to prevent muscle strains.

Many say that the sporting surface should itself be made of a high energy absorbing material. This has been tried with varying degrees of success, but it is clear from the stopwatch that high speeds are not obtained on this type of surface. I conclude that while there is adequate energy absorption at heel strike, there is also so much energy absorption at the point of toe off when maximum power is being delivered to the track that more energy is required to produce the same performance. Furthermore, if some surfaces for ball games were energy absorbing and others not, the predictability of bounce might be slightly affected, interfering with high level competition. Thus, to maintain high standards in sports and improve the level of standardization, producing better competition, it seems more appropriate that energy absorption is designed into the footwear rather than into the surface.

For this to be done effectively, the gait patterns of runners must be clearly defined and the parameters within which energy absorption are required must also be defined. Peter Cavanagh has done some outstanding work on defining the point of foot strike in the running gait cycle and also demonstrating the directions in which the force center travels beneath the foot during the stance phase. These studies have shown great complexity as well as considerable individual variation. Thus, there will be no one running shoe for all runners, and manufacturers must meet the challenge of designing a running shoe not on style but on performance. The high-level athlete may need one type of shoe for training and another for competition.

Particularly hard and unyielding footwear such as racing spikes should clearly have some degree of energy absorption built into the shoe, for not only are high transients generated in such activities as hurdling, but in ordinary track work the deceleration strides at the end of a race produce some of the most bone jarring shock waves that we've ever seen on high-speed cine film. Modern training programs for sprinters often leave out all jogging type of running and work only on strides and sprint performance, never exceeding 200 meters.

From my position in sports medicine I am never too surprised that top-level athletes training in these patterns suffer severe leg and back problems and even get stress fractures in the lower spine. It is essential for responsible sporting footwear manufacturers to provide a service to these types of athletes if they wish to be associated with their results.

With many companies now increasing their sales in response to the boom in leisure sports, it will be their duty to protect all those engaged in sport — from the professional to the once-a-week amateur — from the damage that they know can be prevented to some extent, particularly during training.

In my own specialty we have seen from time to time how traditional orthopedics has been influenced by the sports orthopedic field. Perhaps if sports again leads the way in energy-absorbing footwear, this will spill over to the general population who have no interest in sport. It may give us the first real chance for preventing a host of musculoskeletal degenerative conditions. The recent publication by Voloshin and Wosk in *Clinical Orthopaedics* has shown just how extensive a range of conditions can be influenced by energy-absorbing footwear.

INDICATIONS FOR SHOCK-ABSORBING FOOTWEAR

Perhaps the bottom line of this concept is whether the energy absorption in sports footwear should be mandatory or optional as a basic philosophy. First, certain conditions undeniably relate to the magnitude of stress in the bone. Consider the stress fracture of the tibia, which is widely held to be the result of muscle power in the calf being greater than the ability of the bone of the tibia to withstand the bending force upon it. Some authors believe there is a relationship between the footwear used and also implicate torsional factors from patterns of joint movement in the foot.

Clearly there is much to be done in this field, but we are beginning to find some cases of tibial stress fractures that heal as the result of energy absorption in the footwear while limited sporting activity continues. However, I would not advocate simple energy absorption as a way to heal stress fractures but would suggest that once such a fracture had healed in an athlete, energy absorption should be considered mandatory during all training. With improved design in the future, this consideration can also be applied during competition.

The clear relationship between Achilles tendinitis and hard surfaces has been established for so long that it hardly seems necessary to mention this. But suffice it to say that one professional football club in London has not had a single case of Achilles tendinitis this season, despite an exceedingly rigorous preseason training regime and appalling weather conditions. The trainer clearly relates this to the use of energy absorption in training and competition footwear by his players. One of these players had had two previous unsuccessful surgical decompressions of the Achilles tendon. Yet after only 3 weeks of using Sorbothane heel inserts in his training and football boots he was totally symptom-free and played for the rest of the season without any interruption.

Lightweight footwear that incorporates efficient energy absorbers in the heel would seem sensible for preventing the troublesome subcalcaneal pain of young sportsmen, particularly teenagers who compete or train in indoor leisure centers that are concrete surfaced with vinyl flooring or gymnasts who often generate tremendous heel crashes during their floor work. However, whether this should spill over into their everyday footwear remains an open question. Since Eric Radin has demonstrated that in sheep the skeleton is capable of responding to some extent to shock forces, perhaps it is wise to reserve 50% plus energy absorption for sports footwear and leave everyday walking shoes as currently designed until the relationship between ultimate bone strength and heel strike shock waves is clear.

Modern orthopedic research suggests that skeletal maturity in terms of collagen mineralization generally occurs by the age of 18. Studies of joint stiffness and physical properties of articular cartilage suggest that the quality of this material tends to decline after the third decade. Thus it would seem appropriate that from mid-20s onward, some degree of energy absorption should be incorporated into the construction of all footwear. Particularly those engaged in sports after their mid-20s, I believe, should have efficient energy absorption in their footwear.

TABLE 2   Indications for Use of High Energy Absorption in Sports Footwear

1. Established degenerative joint disease	4. Age over 35 years
2. History of shock-wave induced injuries	5. Diabetes Mellitus
Achilles tendinitis	6. At-risk sports, e.g.
Subcalcaneal pain	Triple jump
Low back pain	Sprint training
Muscle tears	Hurdling
Stress fractures	Javelin
3. History of surgery in load bearing	Squash
skeleton N.B. implant surgery	Tennis
	Basketball

Patients known to be at risk of degenerative joint disease for any other reason should use energy absorption in all their sports footwear, and preferably in their everyday footwear as well. Without exception anyone who has had surgery for Achilles tendon, heel fracture, meniscectomy of the knee, osteotomy of the hip, or conditions such as dislocation of the hip, acetabular dysplasia, or low backache should all have energy absorbing footwear. This should certainly be mandatory for anyone who has had a total joint replacement in the legs. However, I would strongly recommend that no one with a total joint replacement ever indulge in vigorous sports.

The consequence of high activity on total joint replacements are well documented and, even with the most efficient shock absorption, it is hard to visualize implants withstanding the enormous torsional forces placed upon them during strenuous activity. But many leading authorities in implant technology feel that energy absorption in the footwear could help prolong implant survival. One implant manufacturer is now supplying energy absorption as standard equipment along with a knee replacement.

A particular area of difficulty is energy absorption in high-level competitive athletes. Energy absorption in vertical, horizontal, and torsional planes would seem appropriate for middle distance athletes racing and training on tracks with exclusively left curves and generating enormous torsional forces in the mid-right foot. This is vital during all training, and using modern technology can be achieved with minimal weight penalty during competition. There is now some evidence that reduction of heel strike transients might reduce muscle fatigue during competition. Thus, though one would pay a slight weight penalty, improved muscle performance and better running times would more than compensate for this.

Finally, athletes engaged in indoor tournaments where injury in the early stages would be greatly disappointing should all consider efficient energy absorption throughout the competition. Stamina is a function not only of muscle endurance training but also of skeletal endurance. Repeated minor levels of trauma over several days frequently accumulate, causing competitors to be eliminated from the tournament.

One sporting surface not generally considered relevant in this field is the track used for motor racing. Although motor cyclists who frequently ride the surface at high speed and with substantial impact often use extensive padding in their leathers to protect against fractures, race car drivers have not yet introduced those principles into the seat mountings of competition cars to any great extent. Yet the high vibrations and enormous bone-jarring impacts produced by irregularities in a motor race track at 180 mph are tremendously punishing to drivers. This is true not only in competition but also in practice and testing sessions, and with increasingly hard car suspension with downward thrust many drivers suffer excruciating pain both during testing and racing.

Much of this can be eliminated with satisfactory energy absorption. Early studies in Britain on this particular front imply that this will also be standard practice. Who knows but within a few years perhaps standard road cars will acquire this benefit from the sporting fraternity!

In summary, I believe it has been established beyond all reasonable doubt that not only are substantial shock forces generated within the skeleton during sporting and everyday activities, but also that they can be modified by footwear construction. Efficient energy absorption can relieve the symptons in a wide spectrum of musculoskeletal degenerative conditions and protect many athletes from injury to which they would otherwise be prone. Advanced urethane polymer technology has given us materials that can produce energy absorption in footwear of a controlled degree, with a controlled recovery time and high durability, thereby giving the obscure research of 25 years ago clinical reality in the 1980s.

REFERENCES

Alberti, P.W., Hyde, M.L., Symons, F.M., and Miller, R.B. The effect of prolonged exposure to industrial noise on otosclerosis. *The Laryngoscope* **90**:407-413, 1980.

Bertram, J. Stress fractures in Royal Marine recruits. *J. Roy. Nat. Med. Serv.* **56**:78-91, 1970.

Cavanagh, P.R., and Lafortune, M.A. Ground reaction forces in distance running. *J. Biomechanics* **13**:397-406, 1980.

Daffner, R.H. Stress fractures: Current concepts. *Skeletal Radiology* **2**:221-229, 1978.

Frymoyer, J.W., Pope, M.H., et al. Epidemiologic studies of low back pain. *Spine* **5**(5):419-423, 1980.

Hawes, D., Light, L.H., and Repond, E. Modelling the distortion produced by heel strike transients in soft tissue. *J. Physiol.* **296**:10-11, 1979.

Hunter, H., III, Melton, J.L., and Chu, C.-P. Diabetes Mellitus and the risk of skeletal fracture. *N. Eng. J. Med.* **303**(10):567-570, 1980.

Jarviner, M. Healing of a crush injury in rat striated muscle. *Acta Path. Microbiol. Scand. Sect. A* **83**:269-282, *Sect. A* **84**:84-94, 1976.

Jurmain, R.D. Stress and the etiology of osteoarthritis. *Am. J. Phys. Anthropol.* **46**:353-366, 1977.

Kempson, G.E. The relationship between tensile properties of human articular cartilage and age. *Mech. Factors and the Skeleton*, pp. 186-190, 1981.

Leach, R.E., James, S., and Wasilewski, S. Achilles tendinitis. *Am. J. Sports Med.* **9**(2):93-98, 1981.

Light, L.H., and MacLellan, G.E. Skeletal transients associated with heel strike. *J. Physiol.* **9**:10P, 1977.

Light, L.H., MacLellan, G.E., and Klenerman, L. Skeletal transients on heel strike in normal walking with different footwear. *J. Biomechanics* **13**: 477-488, 1979.

Lloyd-Roberts, G.C. The role of capsular changes in osteoarthritis of the hip joint. *J. Bone Joint Surg.* **53-B**:627-642, 1953.

MacLellan, G.E., and Vyvyan, B. Management of pain beneath the heel and Achilles tendinitis with visco-elastic heel inserts. *B.J. Sports Med.* **15**: 117-121, 1981.

Murray, R.O., and Duncan, C. Athletic activity in adolescence as an aetiological factor in degenerative hip disease. *J. Bone Joint Surg.* **53-B**:406-419, 1971.

Peyron, J.G. Epidemiologic and etiologic approach to osteoarthritis. *Seminars in Arthritis and Rheumatism* **8**(4):288-306, 1979.

Puhl, W., and Iyer, V. Observations on the structure of the articular cartilage surface in normal and pathological conditions. *Seminars in Arthritis and Rheumatism* **8**(4):288-306, 1973.

Radin, E.L., Paul, I.L., and Rose, R.M. The role of mechanical factors in pathogenesis of primary osteoarthritis. *Lancet*, pp. 519-521, 1972.

Smart, G.W., Taunton, J.E., and Clement, D.B. Achilles tendon disorders in miners—A review. *Med. Sci. Sports Exercise* **12**(4):231-243, 1980.

Steinbruck, K., and Gartner, B.M. Total hip prosthesis and sport. *Munch Med. Uschr.* **39**:1247-1250, 1979.

Subotnick, S.I. Paediatric aspects of children in sports. *J. Am. Paediatry Assn.* **69**(7), 443-454, 1979.

Segesser, B., and Nigg, B.M. Tibial insertion tendionses, Achillodynia and damage due to overuse of the foot. *Etiology, Biomechanics and Therapy.* Der Orthopade **9**(3):207-214, 1980.

Voloshin, A., and Wosk, J. Influence of artificial shock absorption on human gait. *Clin. Orthop. and Rel. Research* **160**:32-56, 1981.

Voloshin, A., Wosk, J., and Brull, M. Impulse attenuation in the human body. *J. Biomech. Eng.* **103**:48-50, 1981.

CHAPTER FIVE

On Friction Characteristics of Playing Surfaces

H. Stucke, W. Baudzus, and W. Baumann

If we do not consider rocket propulsion, friction is the prerequisite for locomotion on earth. Friction forces are acting in the contact plane of two bodies and thus, one of them being the earth's surface, horizontal forces can be generated. This is true for vehicles, animals, and people. Whenever a body has to be accelerated or decelerated in a horizontal direction, friction plays an important role. There are two types: static friction and dynamic friction. The former is a reaction force in the contact plane of bodies without any relative movement between them. The latter exists only during a relative movement of the contacting bodies, opposing the direction of movement and decelerating the relative velocity.

For both kinds the friction characteristics largely depend on the material and the properties of the contacting surfaces. Depending on type and objective of the movement of the body, different friction characteristics are required. In most track and field events taking place under standardized conditions, such as running, jumping, and throwing, we can observe phases where great horizontal accelerations of the body are necessary (e.g., start, run-up), as well as phases where great horizontal decelerations of the body, connected with a sudden fixation on the foot, is needed (e.g., take-off in jumping, stem-step of the thrower).

In both cases a sliding movement between foot and ground is not desired because it reduces the horizontal ground reaction and dissipates energy. Therefore, a great static friction is required. If by selection of materials and surfaces a sufficiently high coefficient of friction cannot be provided, the use of spikes offers an appropriate solution. Instead of the force-locking connection between shoe and ground we have rather a form-locking connection which allows the transmission of very large horizontal forces. Then the properties of shoe and surface are of minor importance.

However, we face a more complex picture in sport games. A much-larger selection of different movement techniques must be available due to numerous playing situations, interferences with other players, and so on. Sudden accelerations and decelerations are necessary in sports, but very often in combination with turning movements. Moreover, and in contrast to straight-on running and jumping, sliding movements between foot and ground are indispensable. From hence all the frictional characteristics of a playing surface become important, the static and dynamic ones as well. Taking into account the number of people concerned with these problems, the importance of more detailed and objective data becomes evident.

Up to now friction characteristics of sports surfaces have not been investigated very thoroughly. Friction coefficients between different shoes and floors for translatory movements have been published by Prokop (1973), Morehouse (1975), and Nigg (1980) and are also part of tests of artificial surfaces according to DIN-Standards (DIN 18035, DIN 18032). These data are useful for an objective description of the products. The measuring methods, however, being a shear test of material, cannot take into account the real conditions of the human body moving in various sports activities. The influences of the surface properties on the movement technique, and according to that on performance and load, certainly cannot be neglected.

PURPOSE, METHODS, AND MATERIALS OF THE STUDY

The following will present some ideas and results of biomechanical studies, which should contribute to the definition and solution of some problems connected with our topic. The main purpose of our study was to determine some frictional properties of different surfaces during sports activities under real conditions.

Movements

In order to reduce the number of different movements, yet gain valuable information from them, we defined three elementary movements that are easy to perform with a certain reproducibility and are constituents of all complex movements: starting, stopping, and turning. For starting, the subjects were asked to accelerate from a standing starting position to a fast run. For stopping, the subjects were asked to stop a run within one step. For turning, the subjects had to turn their body by about 90 degrees performing a rotation on the forefoot.

Surfaces

The movements were carried out on three different surfaces: an artificial surface typical outside, an indoor surface, and a cinderground surface similar to our tennis courts and still widely used in Germany. To eliminate the influence of different sport shoes, all trials were carried out with the same shoes.

Measuring Methods

The surfaces were fixed on force-platforms and the time histories of the three force components, the free moment, and the point of application of the force were measured and recorded. The friction coefficients have been calculated from the ratios.

$$\mu \le \frac{F_{horizontal}}{F_{vertical}} \text{ for translation and}$$

$$\eta \le \frac{M_{vertical}}{F_{vertical}} \text{ for rotation (turning movement)}$$

All movements were recorded simultaneously with video camera (frequency 60 fps). From the kinematic recordings the beginning and ending of foot movements could be determined.

RESULTS

In all, 100 trials with 5 subjects have been carried out. The results will be discussed by means of characteristic examples.

Starting

Figure 1 depicts the time-function of the vertical and horizontal ground reaction and their ratio. The coefficient of friction is given by the ratio F_h/F_v at defined points of time. The coefficient of static friction is given at the time when the first movement of the foot is detected. The

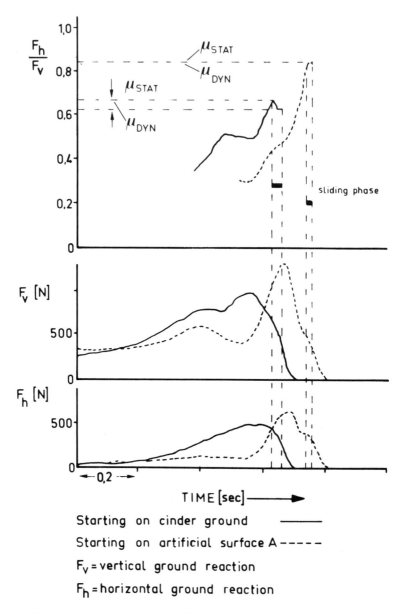

Figure 1 Time function of vertical and horizontal forces and of their ratio F_h/F_v during starting.

coefficient of dynamic friction is associated with the sliding phase. For effective starts, a great value of μ_{stat} is required because great horizontal forces have to be produced. A surface with a small coefficient of static friction yields shorter steps. In order to prevent sliding, the horizontal

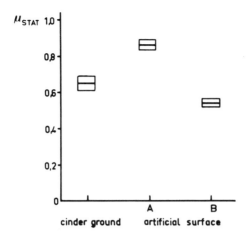

Figure 2   Coefficient of static friction for three surfaces during starting.

forces are kept below certain safe values. In this respect the coefficient of static friction represents the limit of the possible performance of the movement.

During the start, the ground is loaded as long as the inclination of the force remains below a specific value for the given surface-shoe system. If this value of μ_{stat} is not reached, then a sliding phase does not occur during this movement. The coefficient of static friction of a synthetic surface mostly is just the same as the coefficient of dynamic friction, while the dynamic friction on a cinder track is smaller than the static friction.

Comparing cinder ground and surface A, we can see that the value of μ_{stat} of the synthetic surface is higher. This allows a starting position with more forward inclination of the body and greater forces in horizontal direction.

Figure 2 represents the data of 30 trials. It is evident that the values of μ_{stat} for the cinder track range between surface B, which is a typical floor for indoor facilities, and surface A, which is a typical outdoor material. So of course, it is not possible to maintain that cinder track has the lowest friction coefficient or that artificial surfaces can be treated uniformly.

Stopping

Typical force traces of the stopping movement are shown in Figure 3. The coefficients of static and sliding friction were calculated again from the ratio of the horizontal and vertical components of the ground reaction force, except for the cinder track. Because of oscillations in the

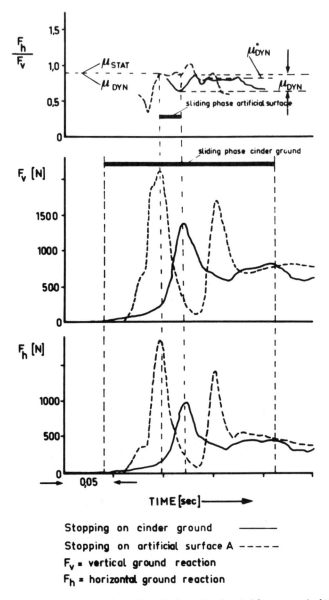

Stopping on cinder ground   ———

Stopping on artificial surface A – – – – –

F_v = vertical ground reaction

F_h = horizontal ground reaction

Figure 3 Time function of vertical and horizontal forces and of their ratio F_h/F_v during stopping.

force-time curve, the coefficient of friction μ_{dyn}^* for the cinder track has been determined at the moment the oscillations end.

For movements with the purpose of stopping a running movement, in practice sliding is only possible on cinder track. On synthetic surfaces we can observe very short spatial and temporal sliding phases which occur after the ground reaction force reaches its maximum. A very interesting difference in the stopping technique on artificial surface and cinder ground can be seen in the force-time functions: The artificial surface allows no sliding and thus forces the subject to unload the ground by flexing the knee joint to render possible a short sliding phase. On cinder ground, sliding occurs during the whole movement starting at the very beginning. Consequently the knee angle mostly remains in constant flexion during the stopping action (see Figure 4).

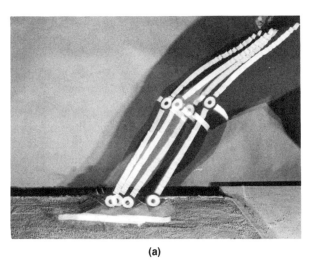

(a)

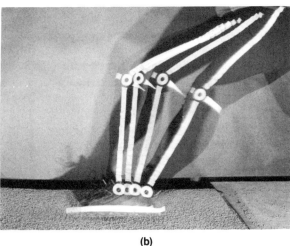

(b)

Figure 4   Strobe picture. (a) stopping on cinder track; (b) stopping on artificial surface.

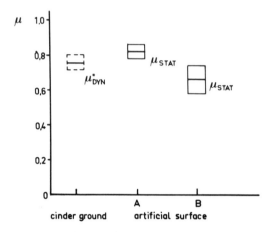

Figure 5 Coefficient of friction for three surfaces during stopping.

Athletes in some disciplines take advantage of this sliding phase (e.g., tennis). If on artificial surfaces this phase is not possible, then it must be replaced by other movements, for example some short steps. It is obvious how far the friction characteristics of the surface influence the sports techniques.

Figure 5 shows the results of all trials for the three surfaces. Again, surface B is smoother than cinder track and the three surfaces are ranged in the same order from rough to smooth (not changed by the shoe).

Turning

Figure 6 shows typical time-functions of the vertical force, the free moment, and of their ratio. As can be seen from the figure, rotation with the foot is only possible when the subject generates a sufficiently great angular momentum of the whole body. In addition to that, it only occurs in connection with an unloading of the vertical reaction below body weight.

This unloading reaches more pronounced values on the synthetic surface than on the cinder track. Without this unloading the angular momentum for the rotation must be much bigger. The rotary motion starts when the angular momentum decreases and the foot is unloaded. It is necessary to produce a specific amount of the angular momentum for a given surface. This angular momentum decreases during the motion of the foot.

The characteristics of the friction of a surface for rotary motion are defined as η, which is the ratio of the torque and the vertical component of the ground reaction force (M_v/F_v). The coefficient of static friction is defined just at the beginning of the foot rotation. On the artificial

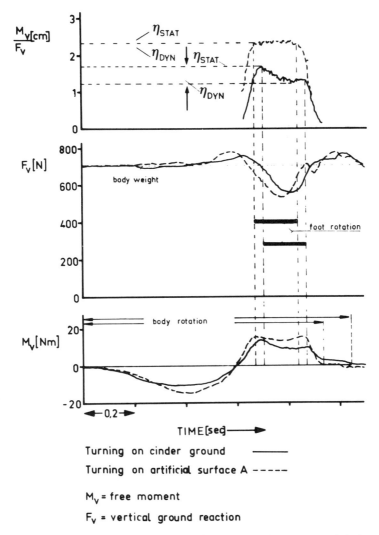

Turning on cinder ground   ————

Turning on artificial surface A ─ ─ ─ ─

M_v = free moment

F_v = vertical ground reaction

Figure 6 Time function of vertical force, vertical moment and their ratio M_v/F_v during turning.

surface, coefficient of friction remains nearly constant during the whole range of motion; that is, static friction equals dynamic friction. On cinder ground, the coefficient of dynamic friction η_{dyn} decreases during the rotary motion of the foot. In Figure 7 the results for the three different surfaces are shown.

The generation of a defined foot rotation on a ground with a higher value of static friction is most probably connected with greater energy expenditure and greater loads on the human body. The more pro-

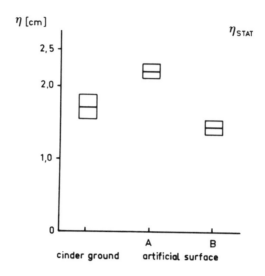

author	motion	friction	Surface		
			outdoor	indoor	cinder ground
Nigg (1980)	translation	static	0,95 - 1,05	1,0 - 1,2	0,4 - 0,6
		dynamic	1,05 - 1,15	1,0 - 1,1	0,5 - 0,6
Prokop (1973)	translation	static	2,5	2,2	2,0
		dynamic	2,4	2,2	1,9
Köln (1981)	starting stopping turning	static static static	0,86 0,82 2,22	0,54 0,67 1,47	0,65 0,76 1,72

Figure 7   Coefficient of friction for three surfaces during turning.

nounced unloading means greater vertical excursions of the center of gravity. Therefore, great values for the coefficients of static and dynamic friction are not desirable for rotary motions.

SUMMARY

The main results of the study are:

- The friction characteristics of artificial surfaces can be very dissimilar, so they cannot be judged uniformly.
- The numerical values of the coefficient of friction for cinder-ground lie between those found for artificial surfaces.
- The friction characteristics of the surface may influence considerably the movement technique. The changes in technique are connected with different muscle work, load on the body, and energy expenditure.

In consequence of these statements, it can be said that the use of surfaces with different friction characteristics is disadvantageous because it requires different movement techniques. It is therefore more difficult to improve a certain technique to a high level and at the same time to develop a repertoire of techniques to meet the requirements of the various surfaces.

The results of this study are of preliminary character. Extension concerning the size of the samples (surfaces, shoes, and subjects) is under way. If it is possible to extract some important criteria to judge a surface or shoe/surface combination, then considerations about corresponding material testing will be appropriate.

ACKNOWLEDGMENT

This work has been supported by the Federal Institute of Sport Sciences (Bundesinstitut für Sportwissenschaft), Köln.

REFERENCES

Baumann, W., and Stucke, H. Biomechanische Aspekte der Beurteilung von Sportstättenböden. *Wissenschaftliches Symposium der DSHS*, 1982, in press.

Bundesinstitut für Sportwissenschaft. Sportfunktionelle Eigenschaften von Tennisplatz-Belägen. *Sport-und Freizeitanlagen*, Bericht B 80, 1, 1980.

DIN-Norm 18032. *Hallen für Turnen unde Spiele*, 1975.

DIN-Norm 18035. *Sportplätze*, 1978.

Haberl, R., and Prokop, L. Die Analyse der Bewegungsbahn um die Stützphase beim Lauf auf unterschiedlichen Belägen. *Österreichisches Journal für Sportmedizin* 2(3), 3-32, 1972.

Haberl, R., and Prokop, L. Die Analyse der Bewegungsbahm um die Stützphase beim Lauf auf unterschiedlichen Belägen. *Österreichisches Journal für Sportmedizin* 2(3), 3-32, 1972.

Haberl, R., and Prokop, L. Über Beschleunigungsvorgänge während der Stützphase beim hauf auf unterscheid lichen Belägen. *Österreichisches Journal für Sportmedizin* 2(4), 1972.

Haberl, R., and Prokop, L. Der Einguß physikalischer Materialgrößen auf die Stützphase beim Lauf. *Österreichisches Journal für Sportmedizin* 3(1): 3-17, 1973.

Morehouse, C.A., and Morrison, W.E. *The artificial turf story*. Penn State, HPER series no. 9:1-62, 1975.

Nigg, B.M. *Biomechanische Aspekte zu Sportplatzbelägen*. Juris, Zürich, 1978.

Nigg, B.M. *Sportplatzbeläge*. Juris, Zürich, 1980.

Stucke, H. Die Beeinflussung der sportlichen Leistung durch Bodeneigenschaften. *Wissenschaftliches Symposium der DSHS*, 1982, in press.

Stucke, H., and Baudzus, W. Der Einfluß der Gleiteigenschaften von Sportböden auf sportliche Bewegungsabläufe. *Wissenschaftliches Symposium der DSHS*, 1982, in press.

CHAPTER SIX

Functional Standards for Playing Surfaces

H.J. Kolitzus

As far as I can see, I am the only engineer among people who deal mainly with biomechanics but not with construction techniques. Thus, the special point of this presentation is sports surfaces under technical aspects.

Before addressing the requirements and problems of testing engineers, a short review on the technical developments of sports surfaces seems appropriate, followed by a report on the instruments that are used to measure the sports functional properties of the surfaces.

In this respect I am familiar with the situation in West Germany, Switzerland, and Austria. In the Netherlands and in France similar activities have been performed, which in France lead to similar results. As for the Netherlands, we do not have exact information on testing techniques, so there is uncertainty about what is going on there.

STRUCTURE OF SURFACES

In principle, all surfaces that are used for sports are sports surfaces. So that includes gym mats, boxing mats, and fencing floors. For our purposes, however, this discussion will focus on surfaces for sports such as basketball or volleyball. It is only necessary to distinguish between surfaces for gymnasiums and outdoor sports facilities. Because of the different climatic exposures, different structural systems have been developed. We shall speak of indoor and outdoor surfaces. I restrict myself to synthetic layers and modern gym floors because they have generated discussion on the functional properties of sports surfaces. Lawns and cinder courts are still optimal in special cases.

TECHNICAL DEVELOPMENT

Until the early 1960s, there was one type of surface for indoor and another one for outdoor application: indoor was the wooden swing floor and outdoor was the cinder court.

These surfaces were produced on the basis of workmanship. The functional aspect was of less interest. These surfaces were suitable for their purpose and the demands of the time. The idea to improve the sports surfaces concerned the outdoor facilities, where cinder courts were subject to various weather conditions. Since this affected the performance of athletes, there was need of a better solution.

For a short time companies experimented with bituminous surfaces. They made asphalt somewhat elastic by adding cork and rubber granules and by modifying the bitumen with oil. The effects of this treatment partly were considerable, but they lasted only a short time. Durability and aging were found to be insufficient.

A breakthrough occurred in the mid-1960s when new synthetic resins became available that could be processed at normal day temperatures, at site conditions, and that had a permanent rubber-like elasticity. The successful use of synthetic resins for outdoor sports facilities also affected the gyms. Companies began to experiment with synthetic resins for gyms, and the so-called elastic gym floors were developed apart from the wooden swing floors.

In practice, the new developments began succeeding around 1968. The Olympic games in Mexico that year saw use of a synthetic layer for the first time in a competition of that international rank.

Many different types of layers have since been developed. This development was characterized by technical difficulties that were introduced by the new materials used. The question of durability especially presented problems. Meanwhile, however, the manufacturers discovered which techniques are suitable for installation of sports surfaces.

Polyurethanes have proven to be the most versatile and reliable synthetic resin. Although initially inferior, polyurethanes were modified systematically so that they now meet all requirements regarding processability and sports functional ability.

Regarding structure, the outdoor sports surfaces can be reduced to the following principal types (Table 1): one-stratum type layers include either massive layer or porous layer; sandwich type layers include either massive surfacing, structural sprayed surface, or porous surfacing. These types of layers are the result of more than 10 years of considering the aspects of economy and function. Economy concerns the application of material and labor optimization of cost-use relation, and function concerns the suitability of the above-mentioned layers in meeting all requirements of sport, climatic conditions, and durability.

In gymnasiums we should distinguish between the following basic types:

- swing floors—structure according to swinging bar principle (crosswise mounted spring boards and load distributing plate) materials: wooden board and particle boards;
- system elastic gym floors—structure according to sandwich principle (elastic basis layer and load distributing plate);
- elastic type surface—structure similar to outdoor surfaces (elastic basic layer and PVC and PUR floor covering).

These surfaces can be distinguished best by their elastomechanical behavior. Swing floors have an "area elasticity" since the surface disfigures itself also in the neighborhood of the loaded point. The resilience of elastic type floors is characterized by point elasticity. This will be explained later.

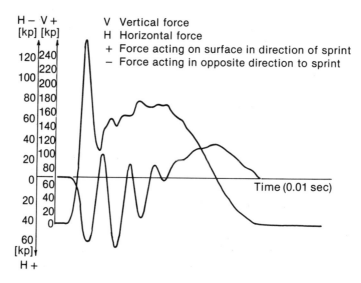

Figure 1   Measurements with Weighbridge middle-distance race.

Explanation:

1 Steel spherical cap
2 Indictive displacement pickup
3 Pressure cell
4 Piston
5 Spring

6 Slide bearing
7 Pulleys to guide falling weight
8 Falling weight
9 Outer tube
10 Steel cylinder with smooth contact area

11 Height of fall
12 Electromagnet
13 Synthetic surface
14 Support (not illustrated)
15 Stand (not illustrated)

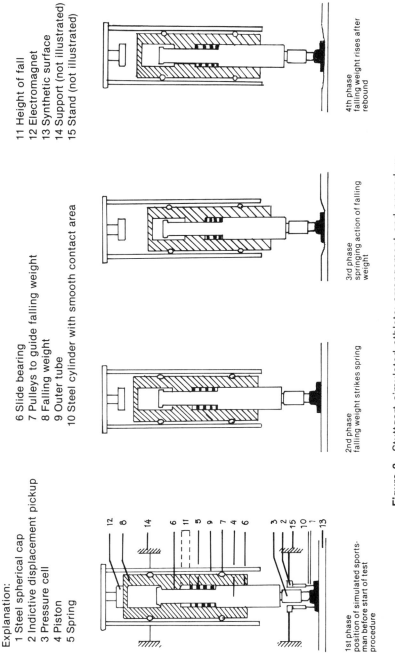

1st phase
position of simulated sports-
man before start of test
procedure

2nd phase
falling weight strikes spring

3rd phase
springing action of falling
weight

4th phase
falling weight rises after
rebound

Figure 2 Stuttgart simulated athlete: arrangement and procedure of test.

101

TABLE 1 An Overview of Synthetic Sport Surfaces for Outdoor Installation

Type of Layer	Structure/Installation Technique	Use	Comments
One-stratum Synthetic Layers (ES)			
Massive layer	layer	Massive PUR-layer with max. 50% aggregate (Elastomergranulat); installation in one or two steps	Track and field High stressed areas of pole vault, high and long jump-running tracks One stratum layers with thickness less than 5 mm	Hard (unavoidable) Image of special qualification for top performance not true Too expensive Development not possible
Typ ES-mk	top	Granular structure achieved by strewing colored EPDM-granules before hardening of the resin of the layer	Impermeable asphalt Climate with lot of snow	
Permeable One-stratum-layer Typ ES-v bzw, sv	layer	Porous elastic layer of PUR-bound elasto-meric granulate In special cases (e.g., Tennis) made of colored EPDM-granulate	Areas for sports games	Discount-construction when black elastomeric granulate is used Renovation of sealing is to be made probably after 2 years Sealings, which are resistant to aging and wear, are problematic in respect to sliding behavior in wet condition

(v)	top	Colored sealing: porous	
(sv)		Or structural sprayed surface rough, depth of profile smaller than 0.5 mm	

Sandwich-type Surfaces (SW)

With massive surfacing (MB)	l.s.	Porous elastic base layer of PUR-bound elastomeric granulate	Track and field events	Sports functional properties (especially resilience) can be controlled by according formulation of elastic base layer and surfacing. As a result better protection function without reasonable reduction of performance
Typ SW-mb	u.s.	Massive PUR-surfacing with topping (colored elastomeric granulate) Thickness min. 1.0 mm		Wearability similar to ES-mk layers
	top	Mostly granular structured by strewing of colored EPDM-granulate (topping) grainsize 1/3 to 1/5 mm		Versatile development possible Much cheaper than ES-mk-layers

Table 1 *(continued)*

Type of Layer	Structure/Installation Technique		Use	Comments
With structural sprayed surfacing	l.s.	Porous base layer of PUR-bound elasto-meric granulate	Track and field events	Very cheap construction Despite relatively small amount of surfacing material rather resistant to wearing
Typ SW-sb	u.s.	Structural sprayed sur-facing mixture of sur-facing resin and colored EPDM-granulate Application min. 1.5 kg/m2		Top structure and sport functional behavior depends on special formulation of spray substance (proportion of mixture, viscosity) and spraying technique
	top	Sprayed structure which results from applica-tion of the upper stratum; characterized by size of granulate and depth of profile according to structure porous or impermeable		

With porous surfacing Beschichtung (HB)	l.s.	Porous layer of PUR-bound elastomeric granulate	Areas for sports games Track and field events in schools	Resistant to wearing and rather spike resistant Surface is very steady despite wearing in respect to view and sports function because of reproduction of surface structure when used Very good evenness of surface if well installed
Typ SW - hb	u.s.	Porous stratum of PUR-bound colored EPDM-granulate thickness min. 5 mm		
	top	Porous, flat; sometimes also rough when additional structured sealing is applied		

105

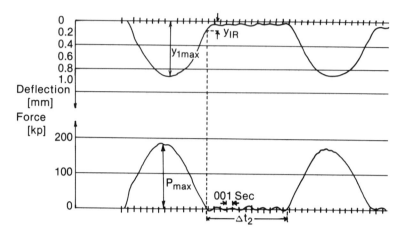

Figure 3 Stuttgart simulated athlete: recording of a test procedure falling test.

In the Federal Republic we disputed which type of floor in principle is suitable for sport functional requirements. All groups have seen that both types of floors do have advantages and disadvantages according to the circumstances of the particular building. Thus, the manufacturers have developed floors that have the structural components of both types of floors in order to combine the advantages and avoid the disadvantages.

Thus, the mixed types have point and area elasticity. We can distinguish the additive method (elastic type floor on top of a system elastic floor), and the differentiating method (stiffness of the load distributing plate is reduced, which reduces the degree of area elasticity). Particularly in the latter method we cannot see an end of the development.

TESTING OF SPORT SURFACES

Development of Testing

Testing of sport surfaces was initiated by the Federal Institute of Sports Sciences (Bundesinstitut für Sportwissenschaften). The Otto Graf Institute (OGI) (Building Research Institute) of the University of Stuttgart conducted the project. In the OGI, I drew up the activities to develop testing instruments that would be suitable to measure the properties of sports functional relevance, and to coordinate all testing activities of the other OGI divisions that dealt with wood, asphalt, and synthetic resins.

We assumed from the beginning that sports surfaces do not have

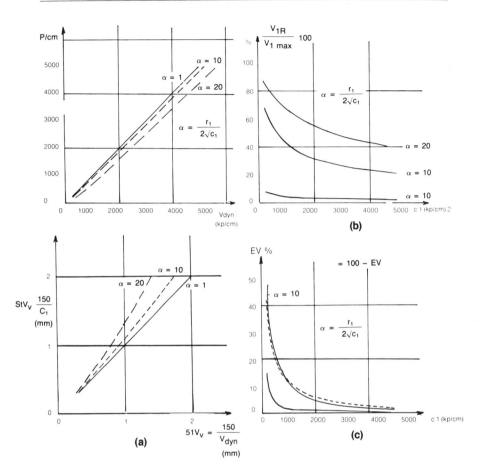

Figure 4 Stuttgart simulated athlete/evaluation. (a) Relationship between the dynamic modulus of deformation V_{dyn}, the spring constant C_1 and the damping coefficient r_1; (b) relationship between the residual deformation y_{1R}, the spring constant C_1 and the damping cofficient r_1; (c) relationship between energy loss EV, the spring constant C_1 and the damping coefficient r_1.

only technical properties. There were many suitable test methods to determine this. We tried to measure the sports functional properties in such a way that there was a certain correlation to the movements of athletes. Because there were no test methods of this type, we had to develop them.

As a basis we had Baumann's results concerning biomechanical measuring. At that time only acceleration measurements had been possible. For designing our new test instruments we needed information about forces, which act between the floor and the foot.

To obtain characteristic force-versus-time curves that occur at

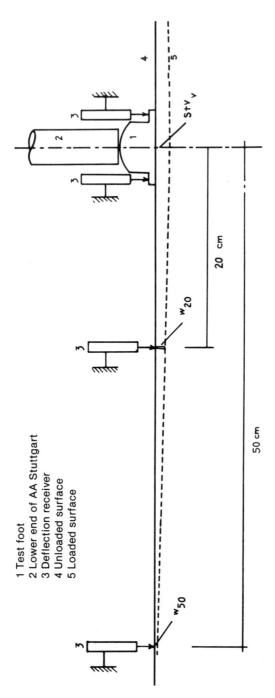

1 Test foot
2 Lower end of AA Stuttgart
3 Deflection receiver
4 Unloaded surface
5 Loaded surface

Figure 5 Measuring techniques for width of deflection using the Artificial Athlete Stuttgart.

Key
1 Impact weight
2 Bounce head
3 Cylindrical spiral spring(s)
4 Force absorber
5 Test foot
6 Guideway for the force meter
7 Electromagnet
8 Lifting device
9 Guideway for the impact weight
10 Support base for the cylindrical
   spiral spring(s)
11 Bounce head/spring/force
   absorber coupling
12 Guideway

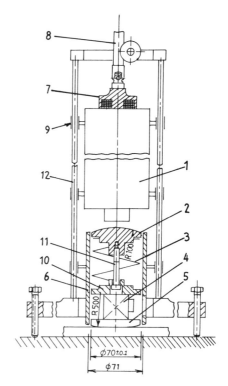

Figure 6   Modified artificial athlete Berlin; structure of the testing equipment (sample).

various movements, we constructed our own measuring slab which was inserted into a track. Although our balance was not as good as that of Kistler we get today, it served our purposes then.

From the diagrams (Figure 1) we can see that the force-versus-time functions consist of two typical parts which can be understood as semisine curves. The first short part is due to bouncing of the heel, and the second part results from carrying over the body.

Thus we developed two instruments to test the resilience, one that had to imitate the hard bounce of the heel and another as a pendant to the second part of the force function. The instruments are called artificial athletes in order to have a popular name for the new measuring technique.

Artificial Athlete Stuttgart

The Artificial Athlete Stuttgart (Figure 2) consists of a drop weight (50 kg) which falls down to a soft spring (50 daN/cm). The drop height is

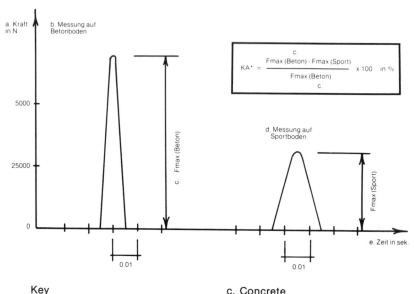

$$KA^* = \frac{F_{max}(Beton) - F_{max}(Sport)}{F_{max}(Beton)} \times 100 \quad in\ \%$$

Key

a. Force, in N

b. Data recorded on concrete floor

c. Concrete

d. Data recorded on sport floor

e. Time, in seconds

Figure 7   Modified simulated Berlin athlete: recorded data.

30 mm. The bounce produces force versus time curves that can be seen on the diagram (Figure 3). The maximum force can be influenced by varying the drop height. In usual tests the maximum force is about 150 daN.

During bouncing the force versus time function and the deformation of the surface is measured. One can see a simple diagram (Figure 4). The resilience is described by the term "standard deformation" StVv. The standard deformation is defined as that deflection in mm which occurs at a dynamic load of 150 daN.

From the diagram we also derive a measure for the loss of energy. The computation is based upon the phase difference. We used the differential equations to compute the loss of energy of the artificial athlete in correlation to the dynamic properties of the floor (spring number, damping number) (Figure 5).

The Artificial Athlete Stuttgart is also used to measure the width of the deflection. The width of the deflection is a measure for area elasticity. The wider the deflection, the more pronounced the area elasticity (Figure 6).

So the depth of deflection is measured in a distance of normally 50 cm from the loading point (axis of instrument). This depth related to the depth in the center of the deflection is a measure of the degree of the area elasticity. When one of the new mixed type gym floors is tested, then W50 is considerably smaller. Then we take the depth at a distance of 20 or 10 cm.

Key
1 Base of testing device
2 Flooring
3 Sole
4 Lower portion of test foot
5 Upper portion of test foot
6 Electrical meter
7 Soft rubber disk
8 Wobble joint
9 Ballbearing fastener
10 Ballbearing
11 Spindle
12 Support flange
13 Frame
14 Weights
15 Winding drum
16 Blocking lever
17 Handwheel
18 Friction bearing
19 Potentiometer for measuring
   the speed of rotation
20 Suspended weight

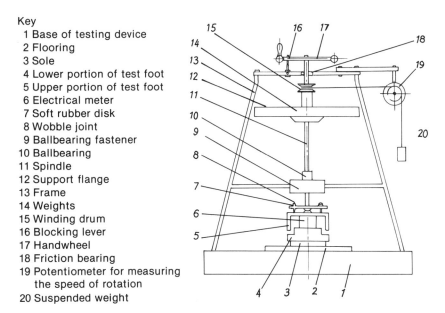

Figure 8   Stuttgart slide testing device: structure of the device.

Artificial Athlete Berlin

In principle the Artificial Athlete Berlin is designed in a similar way as the AA Stuttgart; the drop weight is 20 kg, the spring number is 20 kN/cm. When bouncing the impulse is much shorter than in the case of the AA Stuttgart (0.01 sec on rigid floors). The maximum force is considerably dependent on the resilience of the surface. For a drop height of 55 mm, the maximum force is about 650 daN. On sport surfaces the values are between 200 and 350 daN. When the drop height is 22 mm then the corresponding values are 410 daN and 120 to 220 daN (Figures 6 and 7).

The resilience measured with the AA Berlin is expressed by terms of "force reduction." The force reduction is defined as the maximum force measured on the sports floor related to the maximum force on rigid floors. Thus the force reduction of concrete surfaces is 0%, that of gym mats can be 90%. Gym floors that met the German standards have values between 50 and 70%.

The advantage of this test is that only the force has to be measured. Thus we save time when measuring by avoiding time-consuming set up of the deflection transducers.

Sliding Test Apparatus

The measurement of sliding behavior is performed with the sliding

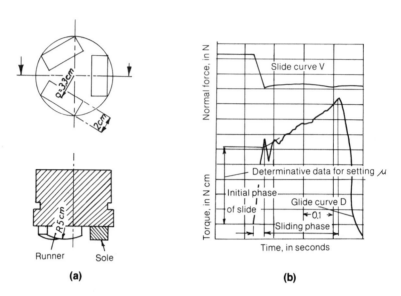

Figure 9 Stuttgart slide testing device. (a) View of test foot; (b) sample recorded data and evaluation.

test apparatus Stuttgart. Here the resistance against movements of shoes caused by friction is measured.

The apparatus mainly consists of a test foot and a spindle (Figure 8). The test foot is mounted centrically at the lower end of the vertical spindle. The connection is flexible. The test foot is put into a revolving movement by aid of the spindle. Doing so, the foot moves downward and touches down moving. Then the foot is stopped by friction between the surface and the sole of the foot. The torque caused by the sliding resistance is measured by transducers mounted inside the foot, which has three skids with leather soles underneath. The sliding behavior is described by the parameter "sliding friction coefficient."

Friction problems are very complex. The sliding friction coefficient depends on the special combination sole material and sports surface. It depends on the degree of abrasion of both surfaces. It depends also on the presence of substances between shoe and sports surface (i.e., dust, water, constituents of the surface). Thus the same surface can be blunt or slippery according to the special condition of the surface (weather, aging, etc.) (Figure 9).

REQUIREMENTS

As far as you may know, requirements for sports surfaces are laid down in the German standards. When the requirements were formulated, it was assumed that sports surfaces have to accomplish three functions: protection, sports, and technical.

The protection function is realized by all those properties which reduce stresses of the athletes during running, jumping, games and gymnastics, and which reduce the danger of injuries during sudden falls. The sports function is the result of those properties that enable optimal exercise of the various types of sports in sports technical respect — as fast as possible, as high as possible, as far as possible, and also as precise and safe as possible. The technical function serves for long duration of protection function and sports function.

The sports function is achieved by the following condition of the surface — resilience. The resilience causes a reduction of the stresses when the foot bounce is placed by the heel, at sudden falls (bouncing with head, pelvis, or joints), at uncontrolled, non-well sprung jumping on the surface.

Bouncing forces arise by braking of the heel or other parts of the body at sudden landing on the surface. The protection function is increased with improved resilience of the surface. The protection function can be realized by the same surface in different situations (placing of the foot, bouncing of the pelvis or a joint, uncontrolled landing) only in a restricted extent in each case.

When the resilience is too extensive, then premature fatigue will result. In this case the resilience is a disadvantage because of the fact that fatigue enlarges the danger of sudden falls and uncontrolled movement. Too much resilience of surfaces with point elasticity causes instability in the ankle joints. This is a danger for the athletes too.

Concerning sliding behavior, if the feet of the athletes cannot turn or slide enough, the athletes are stressed because their feet cannot adjust to changes of the moving directions. When sliding is too easy, there is danger of slipping.

In respect to sports techniques the condition of the surface is sufficient for precise ball action and moving technique. Under this point of view the following properties are relevant: ball rebound, sliding behavior, and resilience. Balls have to rebound well on the surface. Good sliding and rotation of feet improves the athletes' mobility and reduces fatigue. If the surface is too soft, the ankle joints will be unstable and cause fatigue. Unusual premature fatigue affects one's concentration and optimal body action. On the other hand, a considerable amount of resilience will increase interest in sporting.

If one must give a recommendation concerning optimal properties, it is relevant to consider who will use the surface later on. If the surface is used mainly by performance-oriented athletes, the sports functional properties should be preferred. If the surface is to be installed in school or recreation areas, then the protection function has priority because

TABLE 2   A Sample Checklist for Use in Choosing a Tennis Court

General information	Product name	
	Manufacturer/Dealer	
	Product group	
	Scope of uses	
Bottom layer	Type of material (describe substance)	
	Construction of layer	
	Thickness	mm
Top layer	Type of material (describe substance)	
	Construction of layer	
	Thickness	mm
Composition of surface	Type of material (describe substance)	
	Type of surface composition	
	Quantity spread (exclusive of solvent)	kg/m^2
	Total thickness	mm
Supplementary data	Required loadbearing layer	(Loadbearing layer type in accordance with DIN 18035, Part 6, and special features, if applicable)
	Manner of production	(Give figures)
	Sliding friction coefficient, dry	
	Sliding properties, wet	
	Ball-bouncing properties relative to floor surface	W_R % h_R % X_R % B_R %
		Qualitative description including the following aspects: well-groomed/neglected wet/dry new/used evenness of surface texture and condition

Functional properties	Elasticity StV_v	
	Durability rV	
	Aging (changes due to short-term weather exposure)	
	Abrasion	
	Optical and aesthetic characteristics	(color, two-tone factor, luster, cleanness)
	Change of game technique compared with clay court	
	Availability with respect to weather and season	
	Service and maintenance	
Volume of available reference surfaces with a floor of the same type	In production since what year?	
	Location	m^2
	Of these, how many produced by the dealer?	m^2
	Total	
Individual reference locations	Site type	
	Location	
	Produced by which company?	
	Produced in what year?	
Price guidelines, DM/m²	Subfloor construction exclusive of soil planing	
	Flooring without subfloor	
Terms		(warranty, deadlines, etc.)

those concerned are participating in sports for their health and not for achieving best performance. Since most athletes do not have their own gym, those acquiring regulations for sports surfaces must take this special aspect into account.

The three functions of sports surfaces cannot become optimal at the same time because they are contradictory. Thus it is necessary to find a good compromise between the three functions.

Furthermore, one must take into account that sports surfaces are mostly financed by public budgets and therefore their price must be as low as possible. This means that manufacturers must use cheap raw products and simple techniques for installing the surfaces.

FURTHER ASPECTS

You may perhaps regard those considerations about constructional and testing aspects as too simple, but this simplicity was intended. The main task of testing engineers dealing with material and construction techniques of sports surfaces is to see that they are developed in the right direction and that in respect to all points of view the surfaces are built as well as possible.

This means that testing engineers must collect all the facts and evaluate the results of construction technique, sports technique, and biomechanics and to draw general conclusions for the design of sports surfaces.

Sport surfaces are part of construction techniques. In order to achieve improvements in practice as wide and as soon as possible, there is only the means of the construction regulations. Since improvements mostly are linked with a rise in cost and increase of installation technique, both the building owners and the manufacturers try to avoid them unless they are compulsory.

In the Federal Republic of Germany the DIN standards in connection with the regulations for placing public orders are those regulations. The standards are not only acquired by engineers. Competent for this is a working commission, in which all groups interested in the subject to be standardized may take part. Thus, there are representatives of most different interests. The commission for sports surfaces consists of architects, sports experts, merchants, civil servants, chemists, and engineers. Standards can only contain those items that are approved by all members of the commission.

In order to get through here, one must offer simple and clear proposals. It must be possible to control whether a certain surface actually meets the requirements. The test procedures and the derived parameters must in principle be intelligible even to nonspecialists. Most important is the question of test precision; on many sites the properties of the installed surface are controlled. Then a decision is made on whether the surface meets the requirements or not. If it fails, the manufacturer must accept reduced payment or worse consequences. The simpler the tests, the more quickly that test precision can be achieved.

On one hand, the standards are the main means to achieve improvements in quality. But on the other hand, they represent the lowest level of quality if they have been introduced. In addition, there is a lack of information in the standards about the reasons the requirements are formulated just as they are.

Thus, for interested owners, standards contain incomplete information. But how is it possible for them to get better information to make a reasonable decision in a special case?

It is nearly impossible for testing engineers to inform the public about the quality of certain products or to nominate the best surface. This is impossible for technical reasons (which are the relevant criteria in the special case). Yet the manufacturer who fares badly will probably complain and start a legal conflict.

One can only elaborate a check list, which contains not only information on the surface's structure but also on its technical properties (dates of tests), the price, and reference sites. Table 2 shows such a list for tennis court surfaces. The check list is a basis for comparing different bids and to make a rational choice from them.

In addition to this, testing engineers can help the owners of public buildings by promoting a general quality control system. Thus the statistics alone make it unlikely that bad surfaces are offered or installed. In promoting a quality control system, manufacturers should use only proven raw materials and installation techniques. This serves not only the consumers but also the manufacturers in their relations with suppliers.

Having concluded this discussion, I hope the information herein contributes to an appreciation for the technical aspects of sports surfaces.

REFERENCES

Anforderungen an Kunststoffbeläge für Leichtathletik-Laufbahnen
und Anlaufbahnen
Bundesinstitut für Sportwissenschaft, Köln
Schriftenreihe Sport - und Freizeitanlagen B2/73

DIN 18032 'Sporthallen' Teil 1 und Teil 2

DIN 18035 Teil 6 'Sportplätze; Kunststoff-Flächen'

H.J. Kolitzus
Sporthallenböden; Untersuchungsverfahren und Anforderungen
Sportstättenbau und Bäderanlagen 1972

H.J. Kolitzus
Kunststoffbeläge für Spielfelder und Laufbahnen
Das Gartenamt 1977

Sportfunktionelle Eigenschaften von Spielfeldbelägen aus
Kunststoff
Bundesinstitut für Sportwissenschaft, Köln
Schriftenreihe Sport - und Freizeitanlagen B2/80

Sportfunktionelle Eigenschaften von Tennisplatzbelägen
Bundesinstitut für Sportwissenschaft, Köln
Schriftenreihe Sport - und Freizeitanlagen B1/80

Forschungsauftrag 'Mechanisch stabilisierte Tennenplätze'
Institut für Sportstättenbau des Deutschen Sportbundes, Köln

H.J. Kolitzus
Unterböden in Tennishallen
Deutsche Bauzeitschrift, Gütersloh 1979

H.J. Kolitzus
Ebenheit-Nebensache?
Boden-Wand-Decks, Bad Wörishofen 1981

CHAPTER SEVEN

Reflex Stiffness of Man's Anti-gravity Muscles During Kneebends While Carrying Extra Weights

Peter R. Greene
and Thomas A. McMahon

Perhaps the simplest conceivable mechanical model of a man running would include just two elements: a mass equal to the body weight of the man, and a damped spring whose stiffness constant is equivalent to the average reflex stiffness of the man's leg. Under these circumstances, half of the period of vibration of such a damped mass-spring system can be directly associated with the foot contact time of the man during running (McMahon & Greene, 1979).

In a previous paper (McMahon & Greene, 1979) we show that this damped mass-spring model predicts man's reflex stiffness constant during running to be the order of 5000-8000 lbf/ft (73-117kN/m). This prediction is made on the basis of experimentally observed foot contact times from human subjects. However, intuition would suggest that the overall reflex stiffness of the human leg depends on knee angle, foot force, mechanical properties of the running surface, and running speed. Knee angle and foot force are functions of time during running, and therefore only an average reflex stiffness may be defined over a stride cycle.

In this paper, we set the task of measuring the reflex stiffness of the human leg under conditions of constant knee angle and foot force, to

Reprinted by permission of the *Journal of Biomechanics*.

discover how each of these variables affects reflex stiffness separately.

The concept of representing muscles as linear springs is not without precedent. Houk (1976) concludes that controlled muscular action about a joint (such as the knee) is well represented by a "rack-and-pinion" positioning element in series with a spring. The rack-and-pinion can be controlled purposefully by the individual in moving the limbs through large displacements. However, rapid fluctuations in force level imposed by the environment elicit response only from the spring-like reflex system.

Cavagna (1970) concludes that the overall reflex stiffness of man's ankle extensor system is typically in the range from 2300 to 2800 lbf/ft (34-41 kN/m). Furthermore, the damping action of the muscle groups about the ankle implies the existence of a dashpot element (of damping ratio 0.2) in parallel with the reflex spring element (Cavagna, 1970).

One technique for measuring the overall mechanical properties of a muscle system is to link that system to an external mass, spring, dashpot, or any combination of the three, and observe how such external impedances change the dynamics of the system. Bawa, Mannard, and Stein (1976) performed such experiments on cat plantaris muscle. They concluded an overall spring stiffness for the muscle of 42.0 lbf/ft (0.61 kN/m).

In this paper we attempt to determine the overall leg spring stiffness of man *in vivo* by having subjects execute small-amplitude oscillations while standing on an external mass-spring system. Observation of the resonant frequency of this coupled two-mass two-spring system implies a value for man's spring stiffness. The posture assumed by the subject during these oscillations is similar to the posture found at midstance during running. The expectation is that leg stiffness data measured by this technique will be consistent with observed foot contact times recorded during actual human running.

Simple theoretical arguments are presented herein to explain how overall leg stiffness varies with knee angle, and how resonant frequency of this coupled system depends on the external mass and spring. Moreover, the observed existence of both a parallel and an anti-parallel vibration mode of this two-mass two-spring system allows a theoretical estimate of the overall damping constant appropriate for reflex control of flexion-extension of the leg.

MATERIALS AND METHODS

Experiments

The external mass-spring system was realized in the laboratory by supporting a wooden beam at either end, as shown in Figure 1. The

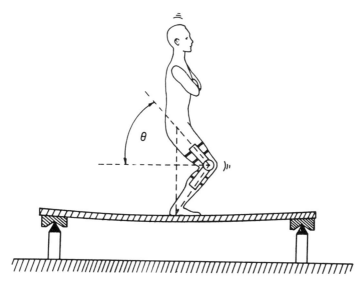

Figure 1   Schematic of a subject executing small vertical bounding motions on a springboard. The knee flexion angle θ is measured with an electrogoniometer. The subject keeps θ near a predetermined value.

knife-edge end supports guarantee that no external moments are imposed when the beam deflects under the weight of the man. Rough-hewn spruce boards measuring 2 x 12 in. (5.08 x 30.48 cm) were used to provide adequate foot area for the subjects. Boards from 7.0 to 18.0 ft (2.13-5.49 m) provided spring constants for this external system in the range from 700 to 10,000 lbf/ft (10-146 kN/m).

The effective mass of these boards, half of the actual board mass (McMahon & Greene, 1979), varied from 0.38 to 1.0 slug (5.56-14.64 kg). Force-deflection tests of the boards showed that such an arrangement behaves as a linear spring for loads as great as 2.5 times the body weight of a typical subject. Loads greater than this invite breakage of the board. For subjects carrying extra weights exceeding this safety limit, two boards were arranged side by side, held together with aluminum cross-braces.

Five adult male subjects were used in this study. Their heights, weights, and ages are summarized in Table 1. For reasons of safety and expediency, not all subjects participated in all trials. For instance, only one subject was willing and prepared to shoulder loads amounting to twice body weight (see Figure 2).

An angle transducer constructed from a one-turn precision potentiometer was taped to the knee of all subjects to monitor average knee flexion during the small amplitude oscillations (Figure 2). Initially, as a training measure, each subject was allowed to observe a real-time oscilloscope display of his knee angle. However, once the subject learned to

TABLE 1   Experimental Subjects

Subject	Age (yr)	Height (ft) (m)	Weight (lb) (kg)	Avg. Stiffness (lb/ft) (kN/m)
T.M.	34	6'3"	170	1350 ± 155
		1.91	77.3	19.7 ± 2.3
J.J.	22	6'0"	192	3250 ± 89
		1.83	87.3	47.4 ± 1.3
R.M.	22	5'10"	180	3053 ± 417
		1.78	81.8	44.4 ± 6.1
J.N.	28	5'9"	174	3790 ± 420
		1.75	79.1	55.3 ± 6.1
D.K.	21	5'8"	150	1450 ± 715
		1.73	68.2	22.1 ± 10.4

Figure 2   Subject J.N. on the springboard, with nearly twice body weight on his shoulders. Note electrogoniometer taped to right leg.

maintain constant mean knee angle during the oscillations, the display was removed from view to avoid the possibility of visual feedback as a factor affecting oscillation frequency. By this technique, all subjects became proficient to the point that angular excursions about average knee angle were held within plus or minus 2 degrees during oscillation.

The terms "knee angle" and "knee flexion angle" are confusing and at times inappropriate. The term knee angle is normally associated with angular measurement made at the knee (angle between thigh and lower leg), whereas knee flexion angle would seem to be the angle between the thigh and the upward extension of the mechanical axis of the lower leg segment. Figure 1, on the other hand, shows θ to be the *thigh angle* (with respect to horizontal). This is perhaps the appropriate term. However, we will use the term "knee angle" herein to denote the angle θ as shown in Figures 1 and 7.

Since vertical foot force at mid-stance during running can exceed 3.0 times body weight (McMahon & Greene, 1979), it seemed important to load the subject with weights of this magnitude to observe changes in reflex stiffness of the leg. This was accomplished by having the subject hold barbell weights at shoulder level (see Figure 2).

Oscillation frequency was measured by timing 20 cycles with a stopwatch. The 20-cycle measurement was repeated three times and then averaged. On occasion, a greater number of cycles were timed, but as these small amplitude oscillations are very demanding on the subject (particularly during the deeper knee bends with added weights), most trials were limited to 20 cycles. It was possible to bounce in such a way that either low frequency parallel-mode oscillations or higher frequency anti-parallel oscillations were excited, but not both simultaneously. The frequency of the parallel-mode oscillation was typically in the range from 1 to 3 Hz, depending on the stiffness of the board in use.

The higher-frequency resonant oscillation of the anti-parallel mode (typically 5-10 Hz) proved too rapid to measure with a stopwatch. For these high-frequency trials, a strain gauge was attached to the board and the oscillation was displayed on a strip-chart recorder (see Figure 6). The amplitude, peak to peak, of the vertical oscillations during the parallel mode was typically 3.0 in. (7.62 cm), with the anti-parallel amplitudes being considerably less (see Figure 6).

The body posture of the subject, to a certain extent, was determined by the physical difficulty of the trial. For modest knee bends (75°-45°) the subject stood on the board with both feet parallel, the heels separated by 8-10 in. (20.3-25.4 cm). Balance became a severe problem, however, for the deeper knee bends (45°-15°). The problem is alleviated by having the subject literally rotate the legs at the hip joint so that the toes point outward approximately 30° to assume a more stable stance.

Except for the extra-weight trials, each subject was instructed to fold his arms rigidly against his chest. This was done to prevent the arms from acting as a third mass-spring system (Harris & Crede, 1976). When this precaution was not taken, significantly lower resonant frequencies were observed.

The subjects were told to exert a minimum amount of effort in maintaining the small-amplitude oscillations so as to prevent oscillating at frequencies off resonance. With determined effort, a subject could force the coupled two-mass two-spring system to oscillate at frequencies either higher or lower than the resonant frequency. After some practice, all subjects learned to execute small oscillations repeatedly with a minimum of muscular effort. The resonant oscillations of the higher frequency anti-parallel mode, because of their tremor-like quality, were not subject to conscious manipulation by the individual. These oscillations occur spontaneously, most often during deep knee bends with weights or after a long period of fatigue-inducing trials.

Theory

Figure 3 is a one-dimensional model of the man standing on the external mass-spring system. The mass m_m represents the man's body weight, and m_b represents the effective mass of the board. The spring stiffness k_m represents the combined effects of muscles and reflexes in the leg. The stiffness k_b is the measured spring stiffness of the board from load-deflection tests with dead weights. The dashpot b represents the velocity sensitivity of the man's reflexes.

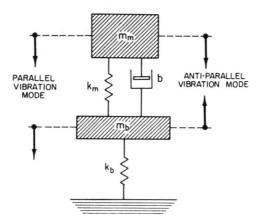

Figure 3 The man and board are idealized as a two-mass, two-spring system in normal-mode vibration. In the parallel vibration mode (low frequency), both the man and the board move downward at the same time. In the anti-parallel mode, the man and the board move toward or away from one another.

Neglecting damping, the resonant frequency of the parallel and anti-parallel vibration modes of this system are given by Den Hartog (1956):

$$\omega^2_{\pm} = \frac{1}{2m_m m_b} \left\{ (m_m + m_b) k_m + m_m k_b \right.$$

$$\left. \pm \sqrt{[m_b k_m + m_m(k_m + k_b)]^2 - 4m_m m_b k_m k_b} \right\}. \quad (1)$$

In equation (1), ω_+ corresponds to the high-frequency anti-parallel resonance, and ω_- corresponds to the low-frequency parallel resonance. Both frequencies are expressed in rad/sec. Most of the experiments are concerned with the observation of ω_- under various combinations of knee angle and body weight.

When finite damping is considered, there is no longer a closed form solution, analogous to equation (1), for the resonant frequencies. Instead, one must resort to the amplitude response curve of the system and locate the resonant peaks by numerical means. This "damped vibrator absorber solution," as it is called, is discussed in detail in Appendix A.

The effect of damping is only pronounced in the lowering of the high-frequency anti-parallel resonance ω_+ (see Figure 5). For modest damping ratios ($0 < \zeta < 0.4$) and board stiffnesses typical of our experiments, damping does not change the resonant frequency ω_- of the parallel mode. This means that equation (1) is still useful for locating the resonant peak of the parallel mode, and that damping can safely be neglected during this calculation. Damping must be considered, however, in the analysis of the high-frequency anti-parallel vibration mode.

Since equation (1) is difficult to solve directly for k_m in terms of the other parameters of the problem, a numerical searching procedure was used to find k_m, given ω_-, k_b, m_b, and m_m.

RESULTS

Man's Average Reflex Stiffness

All five subjects executed small-amplitude oscillations while standing on both feet for knee angle $\theta = 45°$ on four boards of different stiffness. These results are summarized in Table 1. The average reflex stiffness for these five subjects is 3.84 kg/mm (37.6 kN/m), which is close to the average value of 3.80 kg/mm found by Cavagna (1970) for subjects bouncing with locked knees but ankles extended (i.e., plantar flexion). The value concluded for k_m varied slightly from board to board for a particular subject, as indicated by the standard deviations in Tables 1 and 2, but no consistent trend was observed.

Stiffness as a Function of Knee Angle

The results of leg stiffness versus knee angle are presented in Figure 4. The ordinate is rendered dimensionless by referencing k_m (θ) to k_m (45°). In this way, data from different subjects can be presented on the same set of axes. Also displayed are the two theoretical results derived in Appendix B. The dashed line corresponds to the theoretical stiffness of the pin-jointed structure shown in Figure 7. Since this model has a singularity for $\theta = 90°$, it is incompatible with the observed experimental results. The situation is improved by adding another spring element in series with the pin-jointed structure. The result is shown by the solid line in Figure 4.

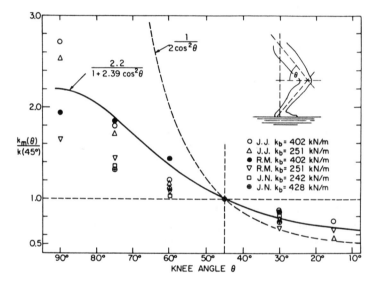

Figure 4   The man's spring stiffness k_m (normalized with respect to the $\theta = 45°$ stiffness) against knee angle. The broken and solid lines are theoretical results derived in Appendix B.

Stiffness as a Function of Weight-carrying and Knee Angle

Table 2 displays stiffness as a function of total weight and knee angle. Total weight is, by definition, the man's body weight plus the weight he carries on his shoulders (see Figure 2). The average stiffnesses and standard deviations quoted result from three trials on each of two different boards. The data indicates a slight trend of increasing stiffness with increasing weight, but this trend is probably not significant because of the standard deviations associated with each data point. (In particular, note the small changes in k_m for subject J.N., who managed to augment his body weight by a factor of 2.89.)

The Anti-parallel Vibration Mode

Extensive tests on the high-frequency tremor-like anti-parallel mode were conducted on one subject (D.K.). The results are summarized in Figures 5 and 6. The solid lines in Figure 5 correspond to the undamped solution ($\zeta = 0$) of equation (1) for $k_m = 16.1$ kN/m. The dashed lines correspond to the theoretical solution of the damped system (see Appendix A) for a damping ratio $\zeta = 0.34$ and $k_m = 16.1$ kN/m. No high-frequency vibration was observed for the stiffest of the four boards.

DISCUSSION

Bouncing on a plank is certainly very different from running. At the outset the expectation was that this controlled form of exercise would exhibit a stiffness constant for the leg in agreement with observed foot contact times during running. Clearly, the average value of 37.6 kN/m (Table 1) falls short of the range 73-117 kN/m concluded by McMahon and Greene (1979) during human running. However, there are several important differences between the bouncing experiments and ordinary running.

First, running is basically a one-legged enterprise, whereas board bouncing, for reasons of balance, is two-legged. Second, during running the knee angle changes continuously, whereas during board bouncing it is held fixed. Third, during running the load changes rapidly from 0 to 3.0 g, whereas during board bouncing it is held fixed. Lastly, running is an oscillation phenomenon which occurs in the frequency range from 5 to 6 Hz, whereas the board bouncing (with the exception of the anti-parallel trials) occurred in the range of 1-3 Hz. In light of these differences it is perhaps surprising that the average reflex stiffness of man's leg during board bouncing falls within a factor of 2 of that observed during running.

However, the board bouncing results can be extrapolated to running. First, to shed some light on the one- versus two-leg problem, limited tests were performed on two subjects (D.K. & T.M.) at knee angle 45° with no extra weights. In order to balance on one leg at this knee angle, the subjects were allowed to touch a supporting structure lightly with their fingertips. On average, the observed one-legged stiffness is 19% less than the two-legged stiffness. This is similar to Cavagna's (1970) one-legged trials, where a 34% reduction was reported.

Second, the average knee angle during foot contact while running

TABLE 2   Average Reflex Stiffness as a Function of Load and Knee Angle

Subject	Total Weight (lb)	Knee Angle (Degrees)	Average Stiffness (lbf/ft)
J.J.	192	0	8546 ± 486
		15	5714 ± 263
		30	3884 ± 157
		45	3252 ± 62
		60	2684 ± 249
		75	2148 ± 366
J.J.	320	0	7321 ± 226
		15	4266 ± 341
		30	3440 ± 156
		45	2771 ± 176
		60	2265 ± 158
		75	2031 ± 299
R.M.	180	0	5452 ± 69
		15	5031 ± 71
		30	3808 ± 190
		45	3053 ± 295
		60	2350 ± 31
		75	2146 ± 41
R.M.	308	0	7457 ± 925
		15	5988 ± 889
		30	4737 ± 88
		45	3380 ± 452
		60	2379 ± 108
		75	2167 ± 110
R.M.	408	0	6597 ± 1213
		15	5590 ± 528
		30	3793 ± 993
		45	2872 ± 291
		60	2092 ± 174
		75	1962 ± 177
J.N.	174	15	5087 ± 490
		30	4073 ± 209
		45	3790 ± 297
		60	2957 ± 353
J.N.	302	15	6546 ± 1099
		30	5031 ± 1092
		45	4322 ± 750
		60	3821 ± 713
J.N.	402	15	6096 ± 1189
		30	5359 ± 1364
		45	5201 ± 1522
		60	4197 ± 888

TABLE 2   *(continued)*

J.N.	502	15	6927 ± 1257
		30	5881 ± 954
		45	5005 ± 1298
		60	3663 ± 792

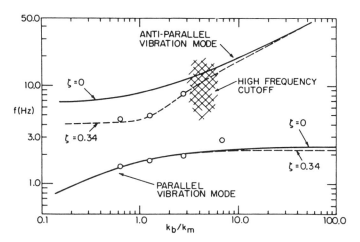

Figure 5   Frequency of vibration vs board stiffness. Open circles show experiments (subject D.K.). Solid line shows theoretical solution discussed in Appendix A with zero damping; broken line shows best-fitting damped curves, $\zeta = 0.34$.

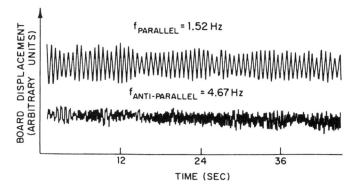

Figure 6   Strain-gauge record of board-bending displacements. The spontaneously-occurring anti-parallel mode has a frequency 3 times greater than the parallel mode. Only one mode was excited at a time.

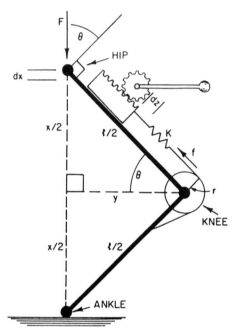

Figure 7 Idealized geometry of the knee and its extensors. The rack-and-pinion represents command signals from higher motor centers. The spring represents muscle reflex stiffness.

is considerably shallower than 45°. Computer-drawn stick figures (McMahon & Greene, 1979) show that at initial touchdown the knee angle is about 75° and at mid-stance it is about 50°. The increased stiffening of the man's leg with shallow knee bends is clearly shown both theoretically and experimentally in Figure 4. In the range typical of running, man's overall leg stiffness is 1.5-2.0 times greater than at $\theta = 45°$.

Third, the extra-weight trials show that leg stiffness increases somewhat with added load at all knee angles. For instance, at $\theta = 60°$, the stiffness at 2.89 g is 1.24 times greater than at 1.0 g (see Table 2).

Lastly, the observed vibration frequency of the anti-parallel mode implies that man's spring stiffness in the 6-10 Hz range is about the same as in the 1-3 Hz range (see Figure 5). In order to reach this conclusion, a damping ratio of $\zeta = 0.34$ was selected as a good fit to the data.

Taking into account the 0.81-0.66 decrease in going from two legs to one, the 1.5-2.0 increase with shallower knee angle, and the 1.24 increase with added weights, one concludes that the average stiffness under running conditions would range from 46 to 76 kN/m. This estimate falls on the lower end of the 73-117 kN/m stiffness range observed during running. In light of the pronounced differences between the two types of exercise, the agreement is quite acceptable.

Another point worth noting is that the average stiffness varies considerably from one individual to the next (see Table 1). We have no explanation for this, other than the subjective impression that the more muscular and physically stronger subjects tend to demonstrate higher spring constants. To a certain extent, this trend is revealed by noting the heights and weights of the subjects relative to their spring constant and their maximum load-carrying capability, as shown in Tables 1 and 2.

The need to include an additional series spring (Appendix B) to explain man's noninfinite stiffness with locked knees deserves comment. The subjects, on average, were only 2.2 times stiffer when standing erect than during a 45° knee bend. A likely explanation would be that the complicated articulated nature of the body allows each of the individual links to flex slightly even though the man makes an effort to stand rigidly on the board. These small motions about a large number of joints tend to decrease the effective stiffness of the body. Also, the thorax and abdominal organs can be thought of as an internally suspended mass-spring-dashpot system which would lower the resonant frequency (Harris & Crede, 1976).

With regard to the high-frequency anti-parallel mode variations, the crucial assumption in matching theory and experiment is that man's spring stiffness and damping ratio remain constant, irrespective of the mode of oscillation. In Figure 5, the values $k_m = 16.1$ kN/m and $\zeta = 0.34$ are seen to match both the parallel and anti-parallel resonances quite well. Under no circumstances were these tremor-like high frequency oscillations observed above 10.0 Hz. This is consistent with the work of Stein and Oguztoreli (1976), where the upper limit for physiological tremor seems to be about 12 Hz. Furthermore, the value of $\zeta = 0.34$, although higher than Cavagna's (1970) $\zeta = 0.20$, is probably a real effect.

The reader can demonstrate this for himself by jumping off a chair onto a concrete floor. When landing with locked knees and ankles extended, it takes several oscillations to bring the motion to a halt. Landing with knees bent, however, is obviously a more heavily damped circumstance. Typically, this oscillation only lasts for somewhat more than one cycle. The damping ratio we found previously for running, $\zeta = 0.55$ (McMahon & Greene, 1979), is somewhat higher than either this result or the one found for Cavagna's (1970) exercise, perhaps because the amplitude of limb motions is larger in running. A similar type of mass-spring-dashpot analysis is done by Rietz and Stiles (1974) in order to explain postural tremor of the limbs of rats.

Finally, Pratt and O'Connor (1976) model a horse's limb as a damped mass-spring system with a damping constant of $\zeta = 0.23$. An important observation is that the damping ratio is substantially less than 1.0 for all three types of exercise.

The data exploring the effect of body weight on leg stiffness (Table 2) indicates a modest but distinct trend of increasing stiffness with increasing weight carried at the shoulders, under conditions of large knee flexion. This trend was particularly pronounced for the subject having previous training in weight lifting (J.N.). Two phenomena, acting together or separately, can explain this effect.

First, it is well known that muscles maintaining an active force and tendons have a force-length relation which shows increased stiffness for increased load. This means that at higher force loads, an isolated muscle-tendon preparation will have a greater stiffness. Second, as muscles bear greater forces, additional muscle fibers are recruited. If each muscle fiber is thought of as a small spring, then additional recruitment means more springs in parallel, and hence a higher overall stiffness.

SUMMARY AND CONCLUSIONS

The effective spring stiffness and damping ratio of the anti-gravity muscles was calculated from the natural frequency of small-amplitude parallel-mode vertical vibrations of a man standing on a simply supported board. The man's spring stiffness for a given angle of knee flexion is essentially independent of the stiffness of the board he was standing on. This result was important because the constancy of the man's spring stiffness was a critical assumption in our previous paper on the influence of track compliance on running (McMahon & Greene, 1979).

The man's spring stiffness was found to be a function of knee angle. A simple theory assuming constant reflex muscle stiffness, and taking into account the varying mechanical advantage of the knee as knee flexion changes (see Appendix B), was in good agreement with the measurements. An additional series spring, representing the distributed spring stiffness of the trunk and upper extremeties, was necessary to achieve this agreement.

When comparisons were made at a fixed knee flexion angle, but with increasing weight carried at the shoulders, the man's spring stiffness either remained constant at small knee flexions or increased slightly at large knee flexions (see Table 2). One subject carried nearly twice body weight on his shoulders; his spring stiffness at the largest flexion (60°) increased by 24%.

Lastly, each subject found that a tremor-like oscillation in hip and knee flexion would occur spontaneously as he stood quietly on the springboard during deep knee bends, more often while fatigued. This oscillation proved to be the anti-parallel-mode vibration of the two-mass two-spring system. From the frequencies of the two modes of vibration as a function of board stiffness, the damping ratio of the damped man's spring (ζ = 0.34) was calculated. This damping probably depends primarily on the velocity sensitivity of muscle and joint receptors. It is midway between the damping ratio calculated for Cavagna's ankle-dorsiflexion exercise (ζ = 0.20) and the damping ratio appropriate for the stance phase of human running (ζ = 0.55) (McMahon & Greene, 1979).

To achieve a quick settling time (time for the controlled output to settle to within 0.018 of its final value) and a modest overshoot, most engineering control systems are designed to have an effective damping ratio between 0.3 and 0.8 (Gupta & Hasdorff, 1970). As a general conclusion, we note that the motor control servomechanisms of the body appear to be under-damped, just as many engineering control systems are.

ACKNOWLEDGMENTS

This work was supported in part by the Division of Applied Sciences, Harvard University, and NIH Grant 1 RO1 AM19638-01 from the National Institute of Arthritis, Metabolic and Digestive Diseases.

REFERENCES

Bawa, P., Mannard, A., and Stein, R.B. Predictions and experimental tests of a visco-elastic muscle model using elastic and inertial loads. *Biol. Cybern.* **23**: 139-145, 1976.

Cavagna, G.A. Elastic bounce of the body. *J. Appl. Physiol.* **29**:279-282, 1970.

Den Hartog, J.P. *Mechanical vibrations.* McGraw-Hill, New York, 1956.

Gupta, S.C., and Hasdorff, L. *Fundamentals of automatic control.* Wiley, New York, 1970.

Harris, C.M., and Crede, C.E. *Shock and vibration handbook* (2nd ed.). McGraw-Hill, New York, 1976.

Houk, J.C. An assessment of stretch reflex function. *Prog. Brain Res.* **44**: 303-313, 1976.

McMahon, T.A., and Greene, P.R. Influence of track compliance on running. *J. Biomechanics* **12**:893-904, 1979.

Pratt, G.W., and O'Connor, J.T. Force plate studies of equine biomechanics. *Am. J. Vet. Res.* **37**:1251-1255, 1976.

Rietz, R.R., and Stiles, R.N. A viscoelastic-mass mechanism as a basis for normal postural tremor. *J. Appl. Physiol.* **37**:852-860, 1974.

Stein, R.B., and Oguztoreli, M.N. Tremor and other oscillations in neuromuscular systems. *Biol. Cybern.* **22**:147-157, 1976.

NOMENCLATURE

F vertical force downward at hip joint (kN)

b overall damping constant of man's leg (kN/m/sec)

dz incremental displacement of the rack and pinion for the quadriceps muscles

f force carried by the quadriceps' tendons (kN)

g acceleration of gravity (m/sec^2)

k spring constant of the man's (kN/m) quadriceps muscles

k_b spring stiffness of the board (kN/m)

k_m overall stiffness of the man's leg including muscles, reflexes, tendons, etc. (kN/m)

k_{NET} series combination of k_s and k_m (kN/m)

k_s series spring added to the pin-jointed model of the man to account for internally suspended masses, compliant joints, etc. (kN/m)

$l/2$ half the distance from the hip joint to the ankle joint while the man stands erect (m)

m_b effective mass of the board (kg)

m_m mass of the man (kg)

r trochlear radius of the knee (m)

y perpendicular distance from the knee joint to the line joining the hip and ankle (m)

ζ damping ratio $b/(2\sqrt{m_m k_m})$

θ man's knee angle relative to the horizontal (degrees)

x distance from the hip joint to the ankle joint (m)

ω_+ anti-parallel mode resonant frequency of the man and board system (rad/sec)

ω_- parallel mode resonant frequency of the man and board system (rad/sec)

APPENDIX A

The Damped Vibrator Absorber

The amplitude response of the system shown in Figure 3 (often called the damped vibrator absorber solution) is given by (Den Hartog, 1956):

$$\frac{x_b}{x_o} = \sqrt{\frac{2\left(\frac{b}{c_c}g\right)^2 + (g^2 - f^2)^2}{2\left(\frac{b}{c_c}g\right)^2 (g^2 - 1 + \mu g^2)^2 + [\mu f^2 g^2 - (g^2 - 1)(g^2 - f^2)]^2}} \tag{A-1}$$

In writing this expression, the following defined quantities are used:

$$\mu = m_m/m_b \qquad = \text{mass ratio}$$
$$\omega_m = \sqrt{k_m/m_m} = \text{resonant frequency of man}$$
$$\omega_b = \sqrt{k_b/m_b} = \text{resonant frequency of board}$$
$$f = \omega_m/\omega_b \qquad = \text{frequency ratio}$$
$$g = \omega/\omega_b \qquad = \text{forced frequency ratio}$$
$$x_b \qquad\qquad = \text{amplitude of the sinusoidal board displacement}$$
$$x_o = P_o/k_b \qquad = \text{static deflection of board}$$
$$c_c = 2m_m\omega_b \qquad = \text{"critical" damping}$$
$$b \qquad\qquad = \text{damping of man.}$$

Expression (A-1) represents the amplitude of the board oscillation when subjected to a driving force given by

$$F = P_o sin \ (\omega t).$$

In general, equation (A-1) produces an amplitude response curve with two peaks, corresponding to the parallel and anti-parallel resonances. The width of these resonant peaks is strongly affected by the damping *b*, with increasing damping tending to widen the resonant peaks. For sufficiently large damping, the two peaks fuse together, and only one resonance is observed.

APPENDIX B

Derivation of Leg Reflex Stiffness as a Function of Knee Angle

By assuming the leg to be a pin-jointed structure, as shown in Figure 7, a closed-form result for the dependence of leg reflex stiffness on knee angle can be found. The knee is represented as a pulley of radius r over which the quadriceps tendons pass without friction. The quadriceps are idealized as a rack and pinion element in series with a spring. The spring is assumed to be linear, with force-length relation $f = kz$. Balancing moments about the knee requires that $y(\theta)F = f(\theta)r$.

While the man assumes a knee bend of angle θ, the rack and pinion is frozen at $z(\theta)$, having stretched the quadriceps' spring k just enough to support the man's weight F. Further oscillatory motion dx causes the spring to stretch an amount dz which increases the forces df and dF. The objective is to relate dx and dF so that we can conclude the overall spring constant $k_m(\theta) = dF/dx$.

The perpendicular distance y from the knee to the line joining the hip and ankle is related to knee angle according to $y(\theta) = (l/2)\cos\theta$. Inserting this fact into the moment equilibrium relation and solving for the equilibrium displacement $z(\theta)$ of the rack and pinion produces:

$$z(\theta) = \frac{Fl}{2kr} \cos(\theta). \tag{B-1}$$

During oscillatory motion about this equilibrium position, we assume that the rack and pinion is frozen at $z(\theta)$ and that further incremental changes in length of the spring are produced only by changes in knee geometry as given by

$$dz = r \, d\theta. \tag{B-2}$$

Neglecting second order terms, the increments in force dF and df are related by

$$y(\theta)dF = df(\theta)r. \tag{B-3}$$

As a purely geometrical result, the change in knee angle $d\theta$ is related to the vertical hip movement dx by

$$dx(\theta) = l \cos \theta \, d\theta. \tag{B-4}$$

We are now in a position to combine equations (B-1)-(B-4) to conclude the overall spring constant of the man $k_m(\theta)$:

$$k_m(\theta) = \frac{dF}{dx}. \qquad \text{(B-5)}$$

Equation (B-3) is solved for dF, and then df and $y(\theta)$ are replaced by previously established relations:

$$dF = \frac{r\ df(\theta)}{y(\theta)} = \frac{kr^2\ d\theta}{y(\theta)} = \frac{kr^2\ d\theta}{(l/2)\cos\theta}. \qquad \text{(B-6)}$$

Taking the ratio of (B-6) to (B-4) yields the desired result:

$$k_m(\theta) = \frac{\left[\dfrac{kr^2\ d\theta}{(l/2)\cos\theta}\right]}{l\cos\theta\ d\theta} = 2k\left(\frac{r}{l}\right)^2 \frac{1}{\cos^2\theta}. \qquad \text{(B-7)}$$

Since we have no direct experimental knowledge of k or r for our subjects, (B-5) is best expressed in dimensionless form:

$$\frac{k_m(\theta)}{k_m(45°)} = \frac{1}{2\cos^2\theta}. \qquad \text{(B-8)}$$

This predicts, as it should, that man's stiffness becomes infinite when he stands erect ($\theta = 90°$). However, our experiments indicate that man's stiffness while standing erect is, on average, 2.2 times greater than the stiffness of a 45° knee bend. Therefore, to resolve the singularity of (B-8) at $\theta = 90°$, another spring k_s is added in series with $k_m(\theta)$. The overall stiffness of this series combination is given by:

$$k_{NET}(\theta) = \frac{k_s k_m(\theta)}{k_s + k_m(\theta)}. \qquad \text{(B-9)}$$

The value of k_s is chosen so that $k_{NET}(90°) = 2.2\ k_{NET}(45°)$ (see Figure 4). Inserting this fact into (B-8) and (B-9) and normalizing, we find

$$\frac{k_{NET}(\theta)}{k_{NET}(45°)} = \frac{2.2}{1 + 2.39\cos^2\theta}. \qquad \text{(B-10)}$$

The physical significance of the series spring k_s is discussed in greater detail in the Discussion section of this chapter.

CHAPTER EIGHT

The Influence of Track Compliance on Running

Thomas A. McMahon
and Peter R. Greene

Running is essentially a series of collisions with the ground. As the animal strikes the surface, its muscles contract and ultimately reverse the downward velocity of the body. Intuition argues that a surface of suitably large compliance is bound to change performance. Running on a diving springboard slows a person down considerably, while running on a trampoline is all but impossible. Our goal in this paper will be to find an analytic expression for the change in the runner's speed, step length, and foot contact time as a function of the track stiffness, and to compare these predictions with experiment.

The simplification that the muscles of locomotion and their reflexes act essentially as springs is supported by recent developments in the study of neural motor control. Reflexes, however, require some time to act—anyone who has unexpectedly stepped off a curb will recall the sharp jolt that results when the antigravity muscles of the leg are not prepared for the impact.

Melvill Jones and Watt (1971) have shown that approximately 102 msec are required for reflex activity from the otolith apparatus to activate the antigravity muscles in humans, so that unexpected falls of less than about 5.0 cm are unaccompanied by reflex accommodation. Even

Reprinted by permission of the *Journal of Biomechanics*.

the simple stretch reflex requires a substantial portion of the running step cycle. The latency of EMG changes associated with automatic responses to a change in limb load are found to be in the range of 79 msec for elbow flexion in humans (Crago, Houk, & Hasan, 1976) and near 25 msec for soleus muscles in decerebrate cats (Nichols & Houk, 1976).

Since the supported period in human running is typically 100 msec, neither reflexes of vestibular nor stretch origin can be expected to participate in the first quarter of the stance phase, and therefore the antigravity muscles of the leg must be principally under the control of command signals from higher motor centers during this time. In the later portion of the stance phase, however, the stretch reflex can be expected to make important modifications of the efferent activity of α-motorneurons. Houk (1976) has argued that muscle stiffness, rather than muscle length, is the property which is regulated by the stretch reflex. He points out that a competition between length-related excitation contributed by muscle spindle receptors and force-related inhibition contributed by Golgi tendon organs could result in the ratio of muscle force to length being regulated, rather than either one exclusively. Support for this view comes from ramp stretches of the soleus muscle in decerebrate cats (Nichols & Houk, 1976). These studies show how reflex action can compensate for stretch-induced reductions in muscle force, thus preserving a linear force-length relation in a stretched muscle that would otherwise show acute nonlinearity. Houk suggests that the action of a muscle (or a pair of muscles) about a joint might reasonably be represented as a rack and pinion in series with a spring.

A modification of this scheme is shown in Figure 1. Movement commands would crank the rack-and-pinion to a new set point for the joint angle, but force disturbances from the outside world deflect the limb by an amount dictated by the damped spring. The dashpot in parallel with the spring is not specifically mentioned in Houk's model, but is necessary to include the rate sensitivity of the stretch receptors and other feedback elements when both muscle force and length are changing rapidly.

Representation of the leg and its musculature as a linear damped spring has already proved successful in describing an exercise in which the subject jumps onto a force platform, falling on the balls of the feet without flexing the knees, and with the ankles forcefully extended (Cavagna, 1970). From the resultant damped oscillation in vertical force (frequency about 3.5 Hz), Cavagna (1970) calculated the effective spring stiffness and damping constant of the extensors of the ankle. The oscillations were always underdamped, with a damping ratio of about 0.2.

In subsequent sections, the function of the damped spring in Figure 1 is separated from the function of the rack-and-pinion. First, under the assumption that the rack-and-pinion is locked, we treat the vertical mo-

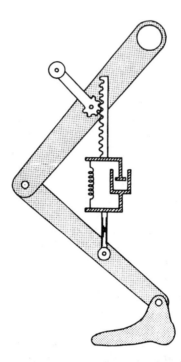

Figure 1 Schematic representing the separate role of descending commands (rack-and-pinion) and muscle properties plus local reflexes (damped spring). The motion of the rack and pinion element determines the influence of track stiffness on step length. The runner's mass and the damped spring determine the influence of track stiffness on ground contact time.

tion of the runner as an underdamped mass-spring system, and calculate the time required to rebound from the track as a function of track compliance. The assumption that the rack-and-pinion is locked emphasizes the local control of muscle stiffness at the segmental level during the middle and late portions of the stance phase of limb motion.

Later, we assume that the damped spring is locked, and geometric considerations are applied to the rack-and-pinion element to calculate the effect of the track compliance on the man's step length. This assumption emphasizes the preprogrammed, nonreflex control of limb position during the early extension phase, before and just after the foot touches the ground.

Finally we obtain a prediction for the top running speed as a function of track compliance. Observations of subjects running on experimental tracks of various stiffness are presented for comparison. Although the calculations show that the man is severely slowed down when the track stiffness is less than his own spring stiffness, there exists an intermediate range of track stiffness where his speed is either unaffected by the track or somewhat enhanced.

METHODS

Experiments

Experimental Board Track. A single-lane running surface 26.25 m in length was constructed of 1.9 cm plywood boards. Each board was 40.6 cm long in the running direction by 121.9 cm wide. The boards were screwed to 4.4 x 8.9 cm rails which served as supports, as shown in Figure 2. The spring stiffness of the track could be altered by moving the supporting rails closer or farther apart. A typical load-deflection calibration, obtained by applying 0.22 kN weights to a 12.7 cm circular aluminum plate representing the foot, is shown in Figure 2b. The time required for the runner to pass between two transverse light beams 8.20 m apart provided a measure of the runner's speed.

The force applied to the track by the runner's foot was measured by a Kissler 9261A force plate, which was linear ± 0.5% over a force range of 0-2.0 kN, and had a natural frequency when loaded with a 70 kg man above 200 Hz. A small 60.9 cm square panel of 0.95 cm phenolic resin board supported at either end by 2.54 cm square pine rails rested upon the force plate, as shown. The separation of the 2.54 cm rails was adjusted until the load-deflection curve of the phenolic board matched that of the track to within 2.0%.

In this way, the runner was presented with a level track surface of uniform compliance, and the vertical foot force could be measured as he struck the phenolic board. Each subject ran down the center of the track to ensure that he experienced the compliance measured by the load-deflection calibration. A 16-mm cine camera, operating at approximately 60 frames per second, provided a photographic record. A clock in the camera's field of view was used to calibrate the camera speed.

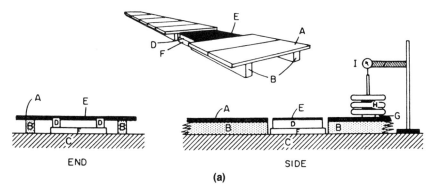

Figure 2 (a) Three views of the experimental wooden track. A—plywood running surface, B and D—spruce supporting rails, C—concrete floor, E—phenolic resin board, F—force platform, G—aluminum plate representing the foot, H—weights, I—displacement gauge.

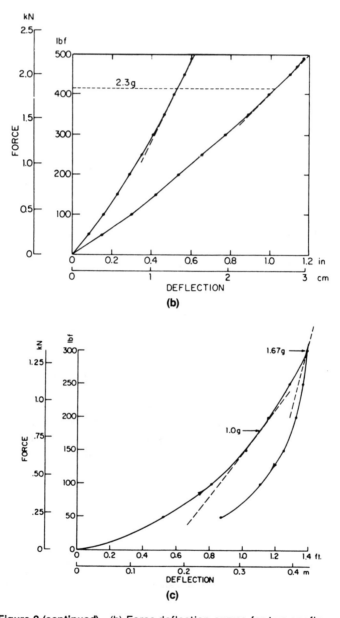

Figure 2 (continued) (b) Force-deflection curves for two configurations of the experimental wooden track. Tangents fit to the 2.3g level
give k_t = 13,333 lbf/ft (195 kN/m) and 6857 lbf/ft (100 kN/m). (c) Force-
deflection curves for the foam rubber pillow track, showing 1.0g and
1.67g tangents, which give k_t = 320 lbf/ft (4.67 kN/m) and 985 lbf/ft
(14.4 kN/m).

A total of 8 subjects, all males between 21 and 34 years of age, participated in the experiment (Table 1). They were told to run at a uniform speed. They alternated runs on the track with runs on the concrete surface beside the track. Each subject ran at a variety of speeds, including his top speed. All runners wore conventional running shoes with thin, flat soles.

Pillow Track.   In order to determine the effect of a very soft surface, the board track was replaced by a 10.9 m long sequence of foam-rubber pillows, each measuring 1.22 m wide by 0.91 m high by 2.74 m long. The runner's speed, step length, and ground contact time on each stride were determined by film analysis. The load-deflection curve for the pillow track is shown in Figure 2c. There was a large hysteresis, resulting in a different stiffness for loading and unloading at a particular force level.

For the purpose of subsequent calculations, the spring stiffness of the pillows was evaluated at two different force levels. This was done by obtaining the local slope of the force-deflection curve at the 0.8 kN level (1.0g), corresponding to foot forces of the order of the runner's body weight, and at the 1.34 kN level (1.67g), corresponding to the mean foot forces to be expected during the foot contact time on this compliant surface. The 1.0g and 1.67g pillow stiffnesses were 4.67 kN/m and 14.38 kN/m, respectively.

Each subject generally was tested at between five and eight different running speeds on each of the four track surfaces (concrete, board track at 195 kN/m, board track at 100 kN/m, and pillow track). There were exceptions, as in the case of the pillow track, where only four subjects participated. As explained in the next sections, foot contact time t_c was included in the tabulations (for Figure 8) only at the highest running speed of each runner on each surface (27 points). By contrast, each step length determination required a straight-line fitting process like that shown in Figure 6. Therefore each of the 27 step length points (Figure 7) represents five or more individual runs.

Theoretical Considerations

Foot Contact Time.   As a general principle, cushioning works to decrease the forces between colliding bodies by increasing the time of collision. Joggers know that they are less prone to ligament injuries and shinsplints when they run on somewhat compliant surfaces such as turf, as opposed to city pavements. Typical stiffnesses of some running surfaces are shown in Table 2.

In Figure 3, a one-dimensional model of the runner and the track is shown which ignores motion in the forward direction and considers only the vertical component. In this model, we have fixed the rack-and-pinion

TABLE 1 Experimental Subjects

Subject	Weight (lbf)	(kN)	Height (m)	Leg Length, l (m)	Step Length, L_o (m)	Hard Surface Contact Time, t_o (sec)	L_o/l	$\left[\dfrac{(\pi/t_o)^2 l}{(1-\zeta^2)g}\right]$	Runner's Spring Stiffness* (lbf/ft)	(kN/m)
M.F.	180	0.800	1.93	1.09	0.896	0.108	0.83	135.1	6781	98.9
N.H.	175	0.778	1.91	1.00	0.814	0.100	0.81	144.3	7683	112.1
T.M.	175	0.778	1.91	1.01	0.890	0.136	0.88	78.8	4084	59.6
J.J.	180	0.800	1.83	0.978	0.878	0.112	0.89	112.5	6474	94.5
P.G.	190	0.845	1.93	1.05	0.896	0.120	0.86	105.2	5796	84.6
J.C.	160	0.712	1.79	0.969	0.859	0.109	0.89	117.7	5919	86.4
S.R.	160	0.712	1.78	0.960	0.890	0.122	0.93	93.07	4725	68.9
G.L.	150	0.667	1.78	0.960	0.878	0.131	0.92	80.72	3842	56.1

$$* \; k_m = \frac{m_m \pi^2}{t_o^2}\,(1 - \zeta^2)$$

TABLE 2   Stiffness of Running Surfaces

Material	Stiffness (lbf/ft)	(kN/m)
Concrete, asphalt	300,000 +	4,376
Packed cinders	200,000	2,918
Board tracks	60,000	875
Experimental wooden track	13,333	195
Experimental wooden track	6,857	100
Pillow track at 1.67g	985	14.4

element from Figure 1 in a single position, thus emphasizing the role of muscle reflex stiffness. The mass m_m is the man's mass, and k_m is the lumped spring stiffness of the muscles and reflexes acting to extend the hip, knee, and ankle. The effective mass of the track surface (the magnitude of an equivalent mass concentrated at a point) is m_t, and the spring stiffness of the track (the inverse of its compliance) is shown as k_t.

In the figure, all the masses and springs are attached so that only that half-cycle of the motion for positive downward displacements of the man (x_m) and track (x_t) corresponds at all with physical reality. When x_m and x_t are negative, the man's foot would, in the actual situation, be separated from the track surface and would therefore not interact with it. Although the permanent connection of the man to the track is fictitious, it makes the mathematics convenient and corresponds approximately to the real situation during the contact portion of the stepping cycle.

Track Mass.   Let us ignore the man's damping for the moment, and consider the undamped vibration of the man and the track. The natural frequency ω_n (rad/sec) of the lowest mode of vibration, in which the two masses move downward in phase, is given by Den Hartog (1956):

$$\omega_n^2 = \frac{(m_t + m_m)k_m}{2m_t m_m} + \frac{k_t}{2m_t}$$

$$- \frac{\sqrt{[m_t k_m + m_m(k_t + k_m)]^2 - 4m_t m_m k_t k_m}}{2m_t m_m}. \tag{1}$$

In the rigid-track limit, $k_t/k_m \to \infty$, $m_t/m_m \to \infty$, and the above expression becomes $\omega_o^2 = k_m/m_m$. In the remainder of the paper, the subscript o will denote the rigid-track limit. In the limit as the track becomes very soft, $\omega_n^2 = k_t/(m_m + m_t)$. The intersection of these two asymptotic behaviors occurs at a track stiffness $k_t^+ = k_m(m_m + m_t)/m_m$, where the natural frequency ω_n^+ is given by

$$\left(\frac{\omega_n^+}{\omega_o}\right)^2 = \frac{m_t + m_m}{m_t} - \frac{\sqrt{m_m^2 + m_t m_m}}{m_t}. \tag{2}$$

A broken line showing the influence of track mass on frequency is shown in Figure 3. Assuming a conventional wooden track construction in which a 1.9 cm × 1.22 m × 2.44 m plywood panel reinforced by 4.4 × 8.9 cm stringers is the running surface, the effective mass of the track is 21.0 kg, which makes $m_t/m_m = 0.25$ for an 87 kg runner. In this calculation, the effective mass of the track is obtained by Rayleigh's method, assuming a sinusoidal two-dimensional mode shape (Timoshenko, 1937). Under these circumstances, the result is that the effective mass is half the total mass of the panel.

The solution shown in Figure 3 including the track mass is seen to be not very different from the solution for the low track mass limit, $\omega_n^2 = k_t k_m/m_m(k_t + k_m)$, plotted as a heavy solid line just above it. For comparison, the solution when the track mass is increased by a factor of 10 is also shown.

Influence of the Man's Damping. Since the track mass encountered in practice has so little effect on ω_n, we consider it no further. Taking $m_t = 0$, we investigate the combined effect of the force-velocity relation in the man's muscles and the velocity feedback in the man's stretch reflexes, represented here by the dashpot element, b, shown in the schematic drawing in Figure 3. From the solution presented in Appendix A, the normalized frequency ω_n/ω_o is plotted as a function of dimensionless track stiffness k_t/k_m for four choices of the damping ratio $\zeta = b/(2\sqrt{m_m k_m})$.

Notice that the damped curves lie above the undamped ones, a consequence of the fact that the dashpot element tends to stiffen the man's impedance in this normalized comparison. The parameter k_m required for this calculation was determined for each ζ from $k_m = m_m\omega_o^2/(1-\zeta^2)$, where m_m and $t_o = \pi/\omega_o$ are the mass and hard surface contact time appropriate for subject M.F. These curves will later be compared with experimental results.

Step Length. Two sequences of stick figures, obtained by analysis of the cine films, are shown in Figure 4. Each figure was drawn by connecting points locating the major limb joints. The topmost point locates the position of the ear. A remarkable observation is that the trajectory of the ear, and therefore of the otolith apparatus sensing head acceleration, is relatively level, whether the subject runs on the pillows or on the hard surface. Both lower extremities and a single upper extremity are shown in the stick figures.

When the subject runs on the pillows, as shown at the bottom, his stance foot sinks into the foam rubber but the swing foot always remains

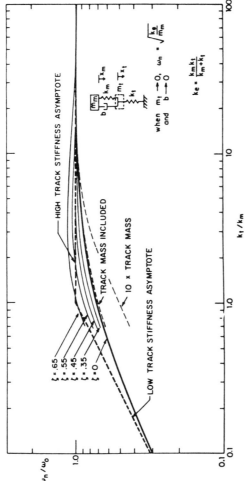

Figure 3 The influence of track compliance on running. Normalized natural frequency vs normalized track stiffness. The inset shows the damped two-mass, two-spring system. Heavy line shows zero damping, zero track mass.

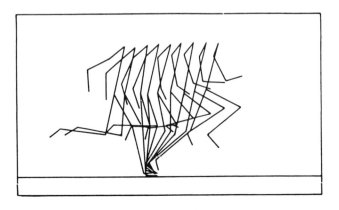

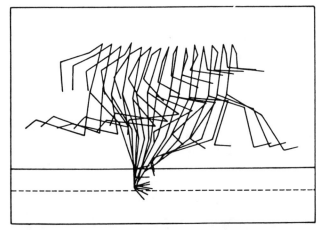

Figure 4 Stick figures of subject M.F. running, from films. Top: hard surface; bottom: pillow track. Solid line shows undeflected surface of pillow track; broken line shows mean deflection of pillows over an entire step cycle. Only those figures for which the foot was in contact with the surface are drawn. The framing speed was 59 frames/sec.

above the undeflected pillow surface. The extended leg encounters the pillow surface in a position when hip flexion is greater than is the case for running on a hard surface. The step length on the pillow surface is consequently greater.

This observation may be used to construct a model for the influence of track compliance on step length. In the schematic diagram of Figure 5 (a), the leg, length l, is shown with the knee fully extended at the moment of contact with the hard surface. It is also shown in mid-stance, when the knee is flexed, and at the end of the stance phase, just before the toe is lifted. In mid-stance, the length of the leg is only $l - \delta_o$, where the shortening δ_o is assumed to be a constant length, independent of run-

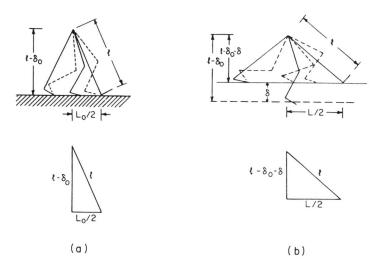

Figure 5 Schematic of a step on (a) hard surface and (b) pillow track. Solid line shows the stance leg, broken line shows the swing leg moving forward. Because the foot descends a distance δ into the pillows, the step length on the pillow track is necessarily greater.

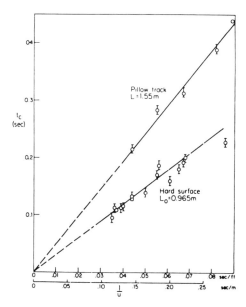

Figure 6 Ground contact time t_c vs inverse running speed $1/u$, for runner M.F. The straight lines through the origin show that an individual's step length is constant, independent of the running speed, on a particular surface. Step length is greater on the pillow track than on the hard surface. Error bars show maximum uncertainty due to film reading.

ning speed, achieved by the "rack-and-pinion" higher postural controllers for the purpose of maintaining the body (and therefore the ear) on an approximately level trajectory.

Notice that this assumption effectively fixes the length of the damped spring in Figure 1 as if the spring stiffness k_m were now taken to be infinite. Since δ_o = 9.6 cm for subject M.F. running on the hard surface, but the maximum deflection of his "spring" would be expected to be only 1.86 cm, this assumption appears to be justified. The important point is that the base of the triangle shown in the lower part of the figure is longer, and thus the step length L is longer on the pillow surface (Figure 5b).

The distance δ is the mean deflection of the pillow surface throughout a complete stride, including the aerial phases. If the man were not running at all, but merely standing quietly on the pillows, he would be standing in a well of depth $\delta = m_m g/k_t$, where k_t in this instance is the pillow stiffness measured at the 1.0g force level. The broken line in Figure 5 (b), representing the mean deflection of the pillow track, plays the same role as the solid line in Figure 5 (a): all details of the step are arbitrarily presumed to be the same, including the distance from the broken line to the hip, $l - \delta_o$.

Only the hip flexion angle at which the heel contacts the track is different on the pillows, leading to the longer step length. Applying the Pythagorean theorem to the triangle in Figure 5 (b),

$$L = 2\sqrt{l^2 - (l - \delta_o - \delta)^2}. \qquad (3)$$

The constant δ_o may be written in terms of the step length on the hard surface, L_o,

$$\delta_o = l - \sqrt{l^2 - L_o^2/4}. \qquad (4)$$

Combining equations (4) and (3), with $\delta = m_m g/k_t$,

$$L = 2\sqrt{l^2 - [(l^2 - L_o^2/4)^{1/2} - m_m g/k_t]^2}. \qquad (5)$$

Equation (5) is plotted in Figure 7 (a), assuming a 0.8 kN man with a leg length l = 1.09 m and a hard-surface step length L_o = 0.896 m (appropriate for subject M.F.). When the expression in the square bracket is zero, the step length has reached its maximum, namely twice the leg length. Thus, running on surfaces whose stiffness is less than $k_t^* = m_m g/\sqrt{l^2 - L_o^2/4}$ would not be possible, according to this model, since the hips would have descended below the surface of the pillows.

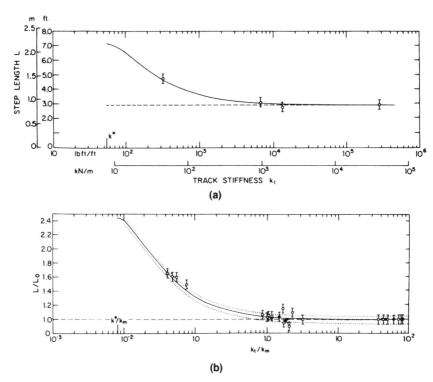

Figure 7   Step length vs track stiffness. The solid line shows the theoretical prediction. (a) Subject M.F. alone; (b) Dimensionless plot showing all 8 subjects.

RESULTS

Dimensionless Plotting

Since the results are presented on dimensionless axes, we have included a short justification for the validity of this procedure in Appendix B. Basically, the method is required because we wish to compare the performances of several runners on the same figure. If the dimensional axes were retained, the performance of a single runner could be compared to a single line especially computed for that runner (for example, Figure 7(a) for subject M.F.), but a complete presentation of the results would require as many figures as there were runners.

Man's Spring Determined by Foot Contact Time

In plotting each data point on a typical dimensionless graph (e.g., Figure 7(b)), it was first necessary to know the man's spring stiffness k_m.

This, in general, is a function of the man's effort and increases as he runs faster. In Figures 3, 7, 8, and 9, we compare only the maximum running performance as a function of track stiffness and therefore $k_m = m_m \omega_o^2 / (1 - \zeta^2)$ where $\omega_o = \pi/t_o$, t_o is the time the foot is in contact with the ground while running at maximum effort on the hardest surface, and ζ is the damping ratio (assumed to be 0.55 for each runner, as explained below).

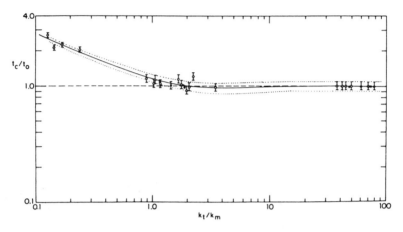

Figure 8 Normalized foot contact time t_c/t_o vs normalized track stiffness, assuming damping ratio $\zeta = 0.55$. Open circles show data produced by film analysis; closed circles show force platform data. Error bars show limits of uncertainty due to film and oscilloscope reading; dotted lines are one standard deviation above and below the theoretical line.

Foot Contact Time Versus Track Stiffness

In Figure 8, foot contact time t_c/t_o is plotted against track stiffness k_t/k_m. The theoretical line represents a damping ratio for the man of $\zeta = 0.55$. This damping ratio was chosen among the four shown in Figure 3, on the basis of its satisfactory fit to the experimental points shown in Figure 8. The linearized spring stiffness of the pillows was taken as the 1.67g stiffness, 14.4 kN/m, since the pillows acted with this stiffness during most of the time the runner was in contact with the track, when foot forces were in the range of 1.67 times body weight. We shall return to this point later, with an explanation of how the figure 1.67g was determined.

The error bars for each point show the estimated maximum uncertainty in reading the films and force records, which was generally less than ±7.0%. The dotted lines on either side of the theoretical line are displaced by one standard deviation σ, where σ is estimated from the root of the mean of squared residuals:

$$\sigma \cong [\hat{\sigma}^2]^{1/2} = \left[\frac{1}{n-2} \sum_{i=1}^{n} [y_i(x) - y(x)]^2 \right]^{1/2}. \qquad (6)$$

Here $y_i(x)$ is the measured value and $y(x)$ is the computed value of a parameter at a given x (Meyer, 1975).

Step Length Independent of Running Speed on a Given Surface

In their comprehensive study of human gait, Cavagna et al. (1976) noticed that the step length, the distance a man travels while one foot is in contact with the ground, is a constant value for a given individual runner on a hard surface, independent of his running speed. We were able to corroborate this finding, as shown in Figure 6 for subject M.F. The time in contact with the ground, t_c, is proportional to the inverse of velocity. The slope of this line defines the step length L, which is independent of the speed but very much larger on the pillows than on the hard surface. When L/L_o is plotted against k_t/k_m in Figure 7, a very good agreement is found with the theoretical line, with a standard deviation of 0.045.

Note that the spring stiffness used for the pillows is now the 1.0g stiffness, 4.67 kN/m, because the deflection δ in equation (3) must correspond to the distance a man would sink down if he were merely standing at rest on the (linearized) pillows. Recall that the step length theory was derived entirely on the basis of geometrical considerations, and did not involve the man's spring stiffness. It is therefore consistent with the observed fact that the step length on a particular surface is independent of running speed.

Foot Force

The average vertical force applied to the ground by the foot during a step is equal to the runner's mass times his mean vertical acceleration,

$$\bar{F} = m_m g + 2m_m v/t_c, \qquad (7)$$

where v is the downward vertical velocity at the moment of contact. In our experiments, we measured v by integrating the force over the duration of t_c, and found no significant difference in v for a given subject on a hard, as opposed to a compliant, surface. Thus v is taken to be a constant, found for a particular runner from the area under the force-time curve,

$$v = \frac{\int_o^{t_c} (F - m_m g)dt}{2m_m}. \qquad (8)$$

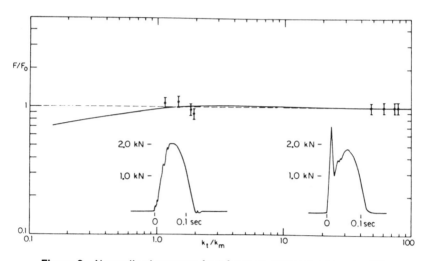

Figure 9 Normalized average foot force vs normalized track stiffness. Solid line shows theory, solid points show average force platform results for each of four subjects. Insets show how the initial force transient experienced on hard surfaces is abolished on the experimental wooden track.

Taking a representative $v = 0.732$ m/sec for a 0.8 kN subject, and using values for t_c obtained from Figure 8 in the case where the damping ratio $\zeta = 0.55$, a dimensionless $\bar{F}/\bar{F}_o$ vs k_t/k_m curve may be plotted (Figure 9). This theoretical line agrees reasonably well with the force-plate data points, and shows that no appreciable change in the mean levels of foot force can be expected until the track stiffness is significantly less than the stiffness of the man. Note that it was not possible to measure foot force during the pillow running experiments, but the prediction would be that average force was lowered to 0.71 times its hard-surface value, or about 1.67 times body weight.

Representative force signatures, traced from the oscilloscope photographs for subject J.C., are shown in the lower portion of Figure 9. On the hard surface, the initial contact of the foot with the ground produced a spike in foot force which often exceeded 5 times body weight. This spike was either absent or very much attenuated when the same subject ran on a compliant track. We suspect this dramatic reduction of foot force at initial contact is the reason that all subjects reported a subjective impression of increased running comfort on the compliant surfaces relative to the hard surfaces.

Running Speed

Having obtained predictions for the ground contact time t_c and step length L, we may put these together to obtain the running speed,

$u = L/t_c$. A consequence of the fact that L and t_c are nearly constant in the intermediate range of track stiffness is that running speed should not be significantly affected until k_t/k_m drops below 1.0. At low track stiffness, foot contact time t_c increases, but so does step length, so the runner is not slowed down as much as contact time alone would predict. For example, running on the pillows increased t_c by an average factor of 2.3, but the runner's speed was not halved. Instead, since step length increased by a factor of 1.6, the runner's speed was preserved at 70% of its hard-surface value.

DISCUSSION

Limitations of the Analysis

It is important to review the assumptions made at various points throughout this paper, and to understand how they limit the analysis. We began by representing the antigravity muscles and their reflexes by the simple mechanical system shown in Figure 1, and used the dynamic characteristics of the spring and dashpot to calculate the influence of track stiffness on ground contact time. Later, we used the conceptual model of the rack-and-pinion element, ignoring the damped spring, to calculate the influence of track stiffness on step length.

We acknowledged the intrinsic nonlinearity of the force-length characteristic of stretched muscle, but claimed, following Houk, that reflex compensation acts to restore linearity. In another paper (Greene & McMahon, 1979), we have measured the short-range spring stiffness of the muscular reflexes of the leg, as a function of both knee angle and total force, and find that the effective spring stiffness of the leg varies by a factor of 2 over the knee angles encountered in running, but most of the variation occurs in the first 15 degrees of knee flexion.

Remarkably, the spring stiffness at a constant knee angle is found to be no more than 25% greater as the subject carries loads up to twice body weight on his shoulders. Thus, as long as the knee angle θ is kept within the range $15° \leq \theta \leq 45°$, as it commonly is during running, our assumption of one single spring stiffness for the leg throughout the step cycle is reasonably valid.

Another simplification involves the pillows: We have assumed that their load-deflection curve is linear, whereas Figure 2 shows that it is most distinctly nonlinear. We have also neglected damping in the pillows, which is probably not entirely justified. In addition, we have neglected the horizontal compliance of the pillows.

We dealt with the nonlinearities of the pillows by assigning the 1.0g stiffness its proper role in determining step length, while we assumed that the 1.67g stiffness determines foot contact time. Since we found that most of the subjects applied a sustained vertical force of about 2.4 times body weight to the hard-surface track, according to Figure 9, $\bar{F}$ on the pillows should be about 0.7 times this value, or about 1.67 times body weight. Thus our measurements and predictions are consistent with our basic assumptions about foot force on the pillows.

Man's Stiffness

The concept of man's spring stiffness is complicated by the fact that it depends on his effort. Under the assumptions of equation (1), when the man runs twice as fast, his spring stiffness increases by a factor of 4. We have attempted to eliminate the effort dependence of the man's stiffness in this paper by making comparisons of performance on different track stiffnesses only when the man is running at maximal effort.

Man's Damping

We employed a damping element in parallel with the man's spring because we knew that (a) isolated muscles obey a Hill force-velocity curve (Hill, 1938) and (b) the muscle spindles return velocity information to the spinal cord. Our decision about how much damping was realistic depended on the curve-fitting procedure shown in Figure 3. Since the curve representing a damping ratio of $\zeta = 0.55$ provided the best fit through the experimentally determined points for t_c/t_o, we took that value of ζ for subsequent calculations of foot force and running speed.

Our assumption that the damping element is linear is certainly a great oversimplification. Katz (1939) showed over 40 years ago that the damping parameter b (Figure 3) is about six times greater for slow lengthening as opposed to slow shortening in isolated muscles. The extent to which this effect is modified by reflex phenomena is unknown.

Could an independent set of experiments, not involving running, be proposed to measure the value of ζ appropriate for running? Cavagna (1970) was able to measure ζ by allowing his subjects to go through several damped cycles of ringing while the muscles of the calf remained in sustained contraction. In running, no such ringing oscillations could ever be observed because the foot remains in contact with the ground for only half a ringing cycle, and the total mechanical energy is the same at the beginning and the end of each supported period. In fact, this is a property of all nonlinear oscillations, that the energy lost in the dissipative mechanism matches the energy added per cycle by the "negative resistance" phenomenon. Thus, only indirect techniques that change the operating characteristics of the oscillator by changing one of its component parts (here we use the track) can serve to analyze the remaining components.

As a final remark it is worth noting that the model of the vertical motion of the runner shown in Figure 3 can easily be made into a nonlinear oscillator. Suppose that when both the man and the track are descending, and therefore when the leg is being flexed by the man's downward momentum, the damping constant of the dashpot, b, is positive, as was assumed in the body of the paper.

As an additional feature, suppose that when the trajectory of the center of mass x_m reaches its lowest point, b suddenly switches sign, and provides negative damping for the next half-cycle. The sudden change in the sign of b requires a sudden advance in the phase of $x_m - x_t$ with respect to x_m, and this requires a step change in the length of x_t. The essential result is that, by postulating a damping which switches sign at midstride (as if it were determined by joint receptors), we may generate an oscillatory motion whose amplitude does not decay with time, and yet whose period is the same as the simple system with linear damping discussed in the body of the paper.

SUMMARY AND CONCLUSIONS

Beginning with a model of the antigravity muscles and reflexes which assumes that they have an automatic, or reactive, component that makes them behave like a damped linear spring, and this is in series with a purposeful component which behaves like an externally controlled rack-and-pinion, we have derived ground contact time, step length, foot force, and running speed as functions of track compliance. These predictions are compared with the results of experiments in which subjects ran alternately on a compliant and a hard surface, and the agreement is generally good.

Very compliant tracks, which have a spring stiffness much less than the man's stiffness, are responsible for a marked penalty in the runner's performance. For example, when a man runs on a track that is 0.15 times his own stiffness, his running speed is reduced to 0.70 times the speed he could run on a hard surface.

On tracks of intermediate compliance, the analytical model predicts a slight speed enhancement, due to a decrease in foot contact time and an increase in step length, by comparison with running on a hard surface. Another important advantage of such tracks of intermediate compliance is the marked attenuation of the early peak in foot force, which can reach 5.0 times body weight in running on a hard surface.

A permanent indoor track having a stiffness about 3 times the man's stiffness has recently been completed in the new indoor athletic facility at Harvard University. Experience to date indicates that good runners are able to better their usual times in the mile by about 5 sec on this track. This represents a speed enhancement of 2%, in good agreement with the theoretical prediction. The runners also report that this track is particularly comfortable to run on, and is apparently responsible for a very low rate of running injuries.

ACKNOWLEDGMENTS

This work was supported in part by the Harvard University Planning Office and by the Division of Applied Sciences, Harvard University, Cambridge, MA.

REFERENCES

Bridgeman, P.W. *Dimensional analysis*. Yale University Press, New Haven, 1931.

Cavagna, G.A. Elastic bounce of the body. *J. Appl. Physiol.* **29**:279-282, 1970.

Cavagna, G.A., Thys, H., and Zamboni, A. The sources of external work in level walking and running. *J. Physiol., Lond.* **262**:639-657, 1976.

Crago, P.E., Houk, J.C., and Hasan, Z. Regulatory actions of human stretch reflex. *J. Neurophysiol.* **39**:925-935, 1976.

Greene, P.R., and McMahon, T.A. Reflex stiffness of the antigravity muscles. *J. Biomechanics* **12**:881-891, 1979.

Den Hartog, J.P. *Mechanical vibrations*. McGraw-Hill, New York, 1956.

Hill, A.V. The heat of shortening and the dynamic constants of muscle. *Proc. R. Soc.* (B) **126**:136-195, 1938.

Houk, J.C. An assessment of stretch reflex function. *Prog. Brain Res.* **44**: 303-313, 1976.

Katz, B. The relation between force and speed in muscular contraction. *J. Physiol.* **96**:45-64, 1939.

Melvill Jones, G., and Watt, D.G.D. Observations on the control of stepping and hopping movement in man. *J. Physiol.* **219**:709-727, 1971.

Meyer, S.L. *Data analysis for scientists and engineers*. Wiley, New York, 1975.

Nichols, T.R., and Houk, J.C. Improvement in linearity and regulation of stiffness that results from actions of stretch reflex. *J. Neurophysiol.* **39**: 119-142, 1976.

Timoshenko, S. *Vibration problems in engineering*. Van Nostrand, New York, 1937.

NOMENCLATURE

b linear dashpot damping constant of man, N. sec. m $^{-1}$

$\bar{F}$ average vertical force during a step

k_m $m_m\omega_0^2/(1 - \zeta^2)$ = stiffness of man's muscles and reflexes acting to extend hip, knee and ankle, N/m

k_t spring stiffness of track (= 1/compliance), N/m

k_t^* $m_m g(l^2 - L_0^2/4)^{-1/2}$ = lowest possible track stiffness for running, N/M

L step length; distance moved during foot contact, m

L_o step length on infinitely hard surface

m_m mass of man, kg

m_t effective mass of the track, evaluated by Rayleigh method

t_c foot contact time on any track, sec

t_o π/ω_o = foot contact time on infinitely hard surface

u L/t_c = running speed

v downward vertical velocity at moment of contact, m/sec

x_m downward displacement of the man

x_t downward displacement of the track

δ mean deflection of pillow surface in a stride, m

δ_o shortening of the leg at mid-stance, m

ζ $b/(2\sqrt{m_m k_m})$ = damping ratio of man

l fully extended leg length, acetabulum to heel, m

ω_n natural frequency of man and track in lowest mode of vibration, rad/sec

Subscripts

m man

o rigid-track limit

t track

APPENDIX A

Calculation of Natural Frequency

Assume the track mass $m_t = 0$ in the schematic drawing in Figure 3. Summing the forces acting on the track to zero,

$$(x_m - x_t)k_m + (\dot{x}_m - \dot{x}_t)b - x_t k_t = 0. \tag{A-1}$$

Summing the forces acting on the man,

$$m_m \ddot{x}_m = -(x_m - x_t)k_m - (\dot{x}_m - \dot{x}_t b). \tag{A-2}$$

The frequency of the lowest mode of vibration, where the track and the man move down together, may be found by assuming a solution of the form

$$x_m = e^{i\omega t} \tag{A-3}$$

$$x_t = A\, e^{i\omega t}, \tag{A-4}$$

where A is a complex constant. Substituting equations (A-3) and (A-4) into (A-1) and (A-2)

$$(1 - A)k_m + i\omega(1 - A)b - Ak_t = 0 \tag{A-5}$$

$$(1 - A)k_m + i\omega(1 - A)b - m_m\omega^2 = 0. \tag{A-6}$$

Subtracting equation (A-6) from equation (A-5) gives

$$A = \frac{m_m\omega^2}{k_t}. \tag{A-7}$$

Substituting equation (A-7) into equation (A-5),

$$\left(1 - \frac{m_m\omega^2}{k_t}\right)k_m + i\omega b\left(1 - \frac{m_m\omega^2}{k_t}\right) - m_m\omega^2 = 0. \tag{A-8}$$

Collecting terms in ω,

$$\omega^3[im_m b] + \omega^2[m_m(k_t + k_m)] - \omega i k_t b - k_t k_m = 0. \tag{A-9}$$

This cubic equation was solved numerically to obtain both the real and imaginary parts of ω as a function of the parameters b, k_t, k_m, and m_m. The real part of ω is called ω_n and plotted in Figure 3 for four choices of the damping ratio $\zeta = b/(2\sqrt{m_m k_m})$.

APPENDIX B

Dimensionless Plotting

The techniques of dimensional analysis allow great simplification and reduction of labor in experimental problems where a large number of variables appear (Bridgeman, 1931). In this paper, two such problems have been discussed, the determination of step time t_c and step length L as a function of track stiffness k_t and other variables. Let us consider the dimensional analysis of each problem separately.

Foot Contact Time

Assume that a functional relationship of the following form exists:

$$f(t_c, t_o, m_m, \zeta, k_t, k_m) = 0,$$

where

t_c = foot contact time, sec

t_o = contact time on hard surface, sec

m_m = runner's mass, kg

ζ = runner's damping ratio, dimensionless

k_t = track stiffness, N/m

k_m = man's stiffness, N/m.

One of these variables, the man's damping ratio, is already dimensionless. From the remaining five variables, the two dimensionless products t_c/t_o and k_t/k_m can be formed. A third dimensionless product using m_m, k_m, and ζ may also be formed, so that the assumed form of the equation becomes:

$$\phi\left(\frac{t_c}{t_o}, \frac{k_t}{k_m}, \zeta, \frac{k_m t_o^2}{\pi^2 m_m (1 - \zeta^2)}\right) = 0.$$

The form of the last dimensionless group was chosen in such a way that its value is unity when applied to any of the runners, according to the definition of k_m assumed in the paper. Thus the functional relationship between t_c/t_o and k_t/k_m may be determined theoretically or experimentally, and applied to any runner.

Step Length

In the calculation of step length, the runner's spring stiffness and damping were excluded from the problem, but his leg length and weight were assumed to be important (his weight determines the average deflection of the track surface over one stride cycle).

$$f(L, L_o, l, m_m, g, k_t) = 0,$$

where

   L = step length, m
   L_o = step length on hard surface, m
   l = leg length, m
   $m_m g$ = runner's weight, N
   k_t = track stiffness, N/m.

The dimensionless form of the equation becomes

$$\phi\left(\frac{L}{L_o}, \frac{lk_t}{mg}, \frac{L_o}{l}\right) = 0.$$

The third dimensionless group, L_o/l, is assumed to be a constant for all runners. The validity of this assumption is reasonably good, as shown in Table 1.

Since k_m is assumed to be a constant, we may write the second group in the form:

$$\frac{lk_t}{mg} = \frac{k_t}{k_m}\left[\frac{(\pi/t_o)^2 l}{(1 - \zeta^2)g}\right].$$

If the term in square brackets is the same number for all runners, then a functional relationship may be found between L/L_o and k_t/k_m, as was done in Figure 7. In fact, this term is evaluated for each of the runners in Table 1. It is not particularly constant, but is greater for the faster runners. The variation in this term explains some of the spread of the data points in Figure 7(b) and shows why comparisons retaining the dimensions (Figure 7(a)) may be preferred in this case.

CHAPTER NINE

Design and Construction of a Tuned Track

David E. Cuin

The research work that has been performed at Harvard University by McMahon and Greene resulted in a number of conclusions reducible to a performance specification which could be used as a basis for the design of a track construction system. Reduced to their simplest form, the parameters defining the required surface were as follows:

- Specified (low) vertical stiffness substantially ($\pm 15\%$) uniform over the surface;
- High level of resilience;
- Low surface mass;
- High horizontal stiffness;
- No transfer of energy between runners through surface;
- Vertical stiffness to be independent of foot contact area.

The reasons for these are quite clear; the lower vertical stiffness at the value determined from the research contributes the reduced injury risk at no detriment to personal performance. High resilience offers a return to the athlete of the energy stored in the surface via its stiffness and deformation. Low surface mass reduces impact stresses in the stance phase of the step cycle while the high horizontal stiffness permits greater tread security and a firm takeoff. No runner should interfere with another during the step cycle by transfer of energy through the surface and he or she should also not experience different running conditions from another athlete due to his or her foot size.

To these factors must be added a second set relating to the construction requirements. These may be summarized as:

- Constructibility—minimum skilled and total labor requirement, minimum on-site time, utilization of typical skills or materials;
- Durability—environmental and functional longevity, control of quality;
- Acceptability—functional and cosmetic;
- Commercial proposition—realistic pricing and profit levels, synergy with company business.

The nature of the En-tout-cas company, which was to construct Tuned Tracks, demanded a high quality, technically sound solution that could be easily transported and constructed anywhere in the world with a minimum of skilled workers and using indigenous skills where possible. It was immediately recognized that most of the requirements could well be served by a prefabricated modular system and the basic design was pursued on this basis. This decision was a key determinant in the form of the final design.

The initial concept envisioned three component areas: a subdivided deck of rigid plates, flexibly connected and suitably surfaced; a resilient, compressible support unit; and a level, firm substructure. Subdivision of the deck into relatively small modular units (4 ft × 2 ft) resulted in an easily handled and economically transported running plate which it was unlikely that two athletes would ever contact at precisely the same time. Such a unit could be cut easily from standard sizes of construction boards such as plywood using techniques common in all parts of the world.

A system of interconnecting tongues was devised that would prevent anything but a level surface between adjacent plates, yet ensure no transfer of flexural energy. The joints between plates would accommodate essential adjustment of dimensions in order to cater for dimensional tolerance in surrounding construction or base and, if they could be exposed, would permit each panel to be prefinished with a factory applied surface if required. In turn, it would offer the opportunity for more rigorous control of quality.

The resilient mountings or shock absorbers were prepared using a specially formulated synthetic rubber vulcanized to metal fixing plates. The disposition and stiffness of these units was determined empirically during subsequent testing phases so as to provide the correct overall stiffness in the final finished system. The substructure could take a number of forms convenient to the location but a level grid of timber battens below the resilient mountings proved one acceptable solution and was used in the first installation.

It was possible in the design stage to incorporate several useful features such as removal of individual deck plates via the track edge for maintenance or repair, provision for heavy vehicle access across the track, and complete demountability. The selected design utilized only four basic hardware components, one rectangular deck plate, and several trapezoidal-shaped plates as segments of bends.

It was decided to utilize a proprietary textured coating of polyurethane and EPDM rubber on the plates in order to produce an accepted cosmetic appearance and provide a tough traction surface capable of readily accommodating running spikes.

Various design prototypes were evaluated and final design was subjected to large-scale loading tests to determine overall performance. Individual components were tested in relation to their function in the surface. Apart from the obvious innovation resulting from the research, this was also to be the first track with a large number of deliberately open joints. Would that be acceptable?

Prototype sprint straight areas were constructed for evaluation by athletes and for outdoor exposure trials. Although these exercises resulted in some "fine tuning" in readiness for the first full track installation at Yale University in the United States, no major change was made in the design.

The deck plates were prepared by a local timber fabrication company using high quality plywood specially produced to a high specification in Oregon. The resilient mountings and all metalware were shipped from England together with the materials for the spray-applied textured polyurethane traction coating, which in this case was to be applied on site.

The construction work at Yale went smoothly despite greater inaccuracies in the concrete substructure than had been specified by the architects. The track was completed on time in the estimated construction time and it satisfied the arthitects' requirements concerning load tests applied after completion of the deck.

The tuned track at Yale is performing up to expectations. Injury levels decreased dramatically in the first indoor season, consistent with observations on the earlier prototype track at Harvard. Running times have not suffered and athletes continue to demonstrate personal best times on the track despite its being unbanked. The fatigue threshold is also raised; the coaches have found it possible to increase the intensity of training without unduly fatiguing the athletes. The joints between the plates seem to present no practical or psychological barriers.

Observations must continue, but the results of this first season appear to bear out the aims of the research. Certainly the constructional efficiency of the design has been proven.

CHAPTER TEN

The Study of Rearfoot Movement in Running

T.E. Clarke, E.C. Frederick, and C. Hamill

Rearfoot control can be defined (in the context of running shoes) as the relative ability of a shoe to limit the amount and/or rate of subtalar joint pronation immediately following foot strike. A normal amount of pronation provides a means of decreasing peak forces experienced by the leg immediately following foot strike, but excessive pronation of the foot can be detrimental in that it produces increased internal (medial) leg rotation and an accompanying stress on the bones and soft tissues. Excessive pronation of the subtalar joint during the support phase of running is linked with various injuries of the hip, knee, Achilles tendon, and foot.

The most common means of quantifying rearfoot movement is by the digitization of high speed film data taken from behind while runners run either on a treadmill or lab runway. By monitoring the position of the calcaneus relative to the lower leg in the frontal plane throughout foot contact, researchers have shown that shoe design, orthotics, and the use of the shoe itself can affect the amount of maximum pronation that is observed.

This paper will review the techniques used to measure rearfoot movement and will summarize the results obtained in order to present a cohesive outline of the baseline descriptive, comparative, and clinical data that already exists. Hopefully, this outline will provide a foundation for future work in the study of rearfoot movement in running.

REARFOOT MOVEMENT DURING RUNNING

The movements of the subtalar joint during the foot contact phase of running have been a subject of concern for many clinicians and scientists who treat and study runners. Pronation of this joint is a complex motion, consisting of simultaneous eversion (turning the bottom of the foot away from the body's midline), abduction (turning the whole foot away from the midline), and dorsiflexion. Supination of this joint involves the reverse movements, or inversion, adduction, and plantar flexion of the foot, respectively (Hlavac, 1977).

A normal sequence of movement for the subtalar joint during running involves a supinated posture at foot strike, after which the foot pronates to a position of maximum pronation, usually within the first 50% of foot contact. The foot then supinates until takeoff. These movements act to decrease peak forces experienced by the leg immediately after foot strike by increasing the time over which the foot becomes stationary on the ground. This range of movement also allows the foot to be a "mobile adaptor" immediately following foot strike and thus compensates for any anatomical abnormalities, such as permanent varus or valgus postures of the leg, forefoot, or rearfoot.

Despite the positive functions of a normal amount of pronation, excessive subtalar joint pronation has been linked with a number of running-related injuries, particularly those of the knee. Clinicians like Schuster (1978) and Subotnick (1981) have found that complaints of knee pain are the most common reason for runners to have to reduce or curtail their running. Hlavac (1977) notes that whenever the heel bone is everted in stance, it is abnormal and usually means that the foot is excessivly pronated from its neutral position. He also states that because the talus is locked in the ankle joint, subtalar joint pronation is accompanied by internal rotation of the leg. Bates et al. (1979) state:

> The relationship between pronation/supination and knee flexion/extension is important since an obligatory tibial rotation is associated with the actions of both of these joints. Pronation and knee flexion are both accompanied by internal tibial rotation while supination and knee extension both result in external rotation. It therefore becomes very critical, especially for people doing a lot of running, that these joint activities be synchronous and complimentary. If maximum pronation and maximum knee flexion do not occur at the same time then the two joints will be functionally antagonistic. If this antagonistic period is prolonged, irritations may result in one of the joints.

Thus it appears that excessive or prolonged pronation can cause knee injuries. In support of this statement, Jernick and Heifitz (1979) showed that the occurrence of chondromalacia (a degenerative softening of the cartilage covering the patella) in 19 female runners was well correlated with a relatively greater amount of subtalar joint pronation exhibited in static weight bearing.

Other common soft tissue problems related to a tendency of excessive pronation are plantar fascitis and Achilles tendinitis (Hlavac, 1977). The cause-effect relationship between this movement and certain running related injuries has made it imperative that a technique be developed that quantifies the amount of pronation exhibited by various runners in different shoes and corrective devices.

METHODOLOGY USED TO MEASURE REARFOOT MOVEMENT

Consumer surveys have been published (Cavanagh, 1981) in which the relative rearfoot control of various running shoes has been rated. To validate such tests, one must actually quantify the amount of rearfoot control that each shoe is exhibiting when used by a group of subjects. Quantification of rearfoot movement is also important in determining the effects of various shoe modifications and orthotic devices which are intended to control excessive pronation. Along these lines, Cavanagh (1981) states, "A standard system of (rearfoot) measurement is needed so that doctors can communicate with each other so that they can measure the effects of various treatments."

The most commonly used means of quantifying rearfoot movement is by digitization of high speed film data. Nigg (1977, 1978, 1980, 1981a, 1981b), Bates (1978a, 1978b, 1979, 1980), Cavanagh (1978), and Clarke (1980, 1983a, 1983b) have, with their co-workers, analyzed high speed movie film to measure the relative movement of the rearfoot and the lower leg, and therefore estimate how much pronation subjects were exhibiting during running at various speeds.

Such analyses involve filming from behind and monitoring the eversion or inversion of the calcaneus relative to the lower leg. Since eversion of the foot is a component of this movement, measurement of the amount of eversion is considered to be a reliable predictor of the amount of pronation that is occurring.

In all studies reviewed, a high speed camera was placed behind the subject to monitor the movements of the lower leg and calcaneus in the frontal plane. Table 1 presents the experimental conditions used to conduct this research on rearfoot movement in running. In all of these studies, two reference markers were used to define the axis of the lower leg and to estimate the relative position of the calcaneus.

TABLE 1 Rearfoot Study Methodology

Author	Film (fps)	Site	Number of Subjects/Conditions	Running Pace Studied (Meters per Second)	Parameters Measured
Bates et al. (1978a)	200	Treadmill	10 subjects/ barefoot, shoes	3.3-4.5	A,B,C,I
Bates et al. (1979)	200	Treadmill	11 subjects/shoes	4.5	A,B,C,I
Bates et al. (1980)	200	Overground	2 subjects/11 shoes	4.1-4.9	A,B,C
Cavanagh et al. (1978)	400	Overground	4 subjects/3 orthotics	4.5	D,E
Clarke et al. (1980)	400	Overground	15 subjects/shoes	4.5	A,B,C
Clarke et al. (1983a)	200	Treadmill	8 subjects/orthotics	3.8	A,B,C,D
Clarke et al. (1983b)	200	Treadmill	10 subjects/36 shoes	3.8	A,B,C,D,E,F
Nigg et al. (1978)	60	Overground	33 subjects/shoes, orthotics	Predetermined stride length	A,G,H,J
Nigg et al. (1980)	100	Overground	40 to 50 subjects/ barefoot, shoes	3.0	A,G,H,J
Nigg et al. (1981b)	80	Overground	40 to 50 subjects/ barefoot, shoes, orthotics	Predetermined stride length	A,G,H,J

Parameter key (see text for definitions)
A. Touchdown Angle (degrees)
B. Maximum Pronation Angle (degrees
C. Time to Maximum Pronation (milliseconds)
D. Total Rearfoot Movement (degrees)
E. Maximum Pronation Velocity (degrees per second)
F. Time to Maximum Velocity (milliseconds)
G. Achilles Tendon Angle (degrees)
H. Achilles Tendon Movement (degrees)
I. Period of Pronation (percentage)
J. Takeoff Angle (degrees)

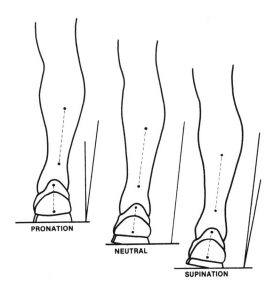

Figure 1 Rearfoot angle measurement. Tracings from high speed film showing rearfoot angle changes during foot contact. Right leg shown from the rear. In this reference system, positive angles between the rearfoot and lower leg indicate a supinated position of the foot and negative angles indicate a pronated position. An angle of zero degrees represents a neutral position.

REFERENCE SYSTEMS

The process of tracking the movement of reference markers in each frame is known as digitization. In rearfoot studies, the four reference markers are digitized and the X-Y coordinate values for these points are somehow stored for each frame of film taken during the foot contact phase. In the reference scheme used in studies by Clarke et al. and Cavanagh et al., the angles that these lines form with the vertical are calculated by appropriate computer software and then compared (Figure 1). The difference between these angles is then termed the rearfoot angle; negative represents pronation and positive represents supination. In their studies, Bates et al. essentially use this system except that they report pronation angles as positive and supination angles as negative.

In his works, Nigg and his research teams have calculated a "heel bone" angle from the medial horizontal plane, and an Achilles tendon (rearfoot angle) as the angle between the heel and leg angles on the medial side. Thus, for the sake of comparison, when Nigg reports an Achilles tendon angle of 192 degrees, this is comparable to a −12 degree angle in the Cavanagh/Clarke scheme, and a +12 degree angle in the Bates scheme. Although all these reference systems are equally good, for the sake of simplicity all results of any study discussed in this paper will be converted to the Cavanagh/Clarke system.

Determining Calcaneus Movement

Bates et al. (1978a) and Nigg et al. (1980) have presented rearfoot data on subjects running barefoot. In these studies, calcaneus eversion or inversion was easily monitored since two reference markers could be placed directly upon the midline of this bone. A problem arises when studying the rearfoot movement exhibited by subjects running in shoes, since the midline of the calcaneus must be estimated from two markers placed vertically on the rear of the shoe (Figure 1). The question arises as to whether or not the calcaneus and the heel counter of the shoe have the same movements.

In answer to this, both Clarke et al. (1980) and Nigg et al. (1981b) have conducted studies with small sample sizes using windows cut in the rear of test shoes in order to compare the movement of the heel and shoe. They have shown that the markers placed on the shoe move in a very similar pattern to those on the rear of the calcaneus. This information is encouraging in that it indicates that the method of following the movement of markers placed on the shoe's heel counter in order to determine rearfoot movement is valid.

Despite this information, when conducting a rearfoot experiment one must be aware of the fact that the shoe must fit the subject well in the heel area in order to expect shoe and heel movements to be well correlated. Also, while some might argue that experimenters should cut windows in or use clear heel counters to study rearfoot movement, such modifications probably will affect the very rearfoot control properties that are being tested. At present, the method of marking the heel counters appears to be the best means available.

A problem that can arise is that of a constant offset between the midline of the calcaneus and the markers defining the midline of the shoe's heel counter. This will affect the results obtained as illustrated in Figure 2. As an example, suppose that two subjects put on the same experimental shoe. Due to anatomical differences that affect the fit, the heel might be oriented differently, relative to the heel counter in each case. As shown in Figure 2, throughout foot contact these subjects would show a consistent offset of 5 degrees, despite the fact that anatomically they were exhibiting the same range of movement. If one is reporting relative rearfoot movement (Cavanagh et al., 1978; Nigg et al., 1980; Clarke et al., 1983a, 1983b), then this offset is not a problem.

However, such a situation does affect results given in absolute terms of degrees of supination or pronation unless some attempt is made to normalize heel angle position. Cavanagh et al. (1978) state, "A further

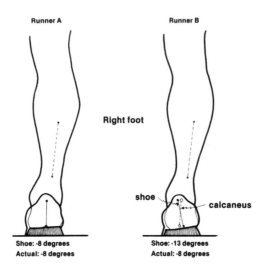

Figure 2 Shoe orientation can affect pronation values as illustrated in this diagram. In both cases, the actual angle of the calcaneus midline to the lower leg is −8 degrees.

reason for using the quantity (relative rearfoot movement) is that the insertion of an orthotic would be expected to change the shoe angle just prior to initial contact even if the true joint angle remained the same as the control condition."

In a recent study (Clarke et al., 1983b) we used a calibration so that absolute as well as relative measures could be made. Before each run in a different shoe began, the subjects were filmed for a calibration shot in which they stood with each foot abducted 7 degrees and their heels 5 centimeters apart. The repeatability of this stance was guaranteed by the use of a wooden blocker which guided foot placement. Heel angles were then calculated for this static posture, and the difference from the vertical was subtracted from all heel angles obtained dynamically.

It was felt that this was the best way to standardize heel angle markings on the shoe as this technique normalizes the heel angle to the vertical during static weight bearing. Over 360 subject/shoe conditions, it was found that these calibration angles averaged 1.2 degrees, and varied from 0 to 4.2 degrees.

A similar method had been previously used by Clarke et al. (1980). None of the other studies reviewed made mention of the use of such a procedure. Although the calibration angle is obtained from a static and not dynamic posture, this would seem at present to be the best calibration that can be made. From the magnitudes obtained for calibration values, it would appear that anyone reporting absolute values for supination and pronation should use some type of normalization scheme.

Determining Leg Movement

Although there is never a problem with seeing the reference markers placed on the leg, care must be taken to insure that a line connecting the two markers is indeed parallel to the long axis of the lower leg. Markers that are not placed consistently will produce an offset which reduces the day-to-day repeatability and affects absolute supination and pronation values in a manner similar to that previously explained for the heel angle. Again, none of the studies reviewed has mentioned the potential problem. However, unlike the heel angle, it is not possible to use a leg calibration angle taken from film because individuals have different amounts of tibial angulation, and correcting this angle to the vertical would be anatomically misleading.

In order to obtain repeatable and reliable leg marker placement, we have recently used the following system: Reference markers are placed on the rear of each subject's lower leg 20 cm apart. The lower marker is centered on the Achilles tendon, while the top marker is placed below the gastrocnemius, and oriented so that a line connecting the two points is parallel to the axis of the lower leg. In order to have a consistent method for determining the lower leg axis, an adjustable clamp was made which, when placed around the knee joint from behind, allowed the determination of the geometric center of this joint in the frontal plane.

A string was then drawn from that point to the center of the Achilles tendon and the upper marker was along the connecting line. It is felt that this system allows day-to-day comparisons of results on the same subject. Such comparisons are risky at best when the leg axis is "eye-balled."

Parameters Measured

Various rearfoot parameters have been examined by different researchers. A rearfoot angle curve from foot strike until 150 milliseconds after foot strike is shown in Figure 3. This was a pattern exhibited by a subject running on the treadmill at 7 minutes per mile. Similar curves have been presented in studies by Bates et al. (1978a & b), Cavanagh et al. (1978), and Nigg et al. (1981a). Some parameters of interest that are illustrated by this curve are the following: (a) touchdown angle — the angle of the heel relative to the leg at footstrike; (b) maximum pronation angle — the greatest amount of pronation exhibited during foot contact; (c) time to maximum pronation — the time elapsed between foot strike and when pronation occurs; (d) total rearfoot movement — this value is obtained by adding the absolute values of the touchdown and maximum pronation angles.

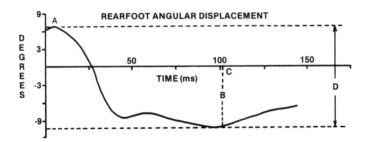

Figure 3 Rearfoot angle curve from a selected subject (Clarke et al., 1983b) beginning at footstrike and continuing for 150 milliseconds of heel contact. Parameters measured from these data are: A) touchdown angle, B) maximum pronation angle, C) time to maximum pronation and D) total rearfoot movement.

From a rearfoot angular velocity curve (Figure 4) obtained by differentiating the displacement data shown in Figure 3, the parameters that were examined are: (e) maximum pronation velocity—the peak angular velocity exhibited by the rearfoot during foot contact; and (f) time to maximum velocity—the time elapsed between foot strike and when maximum pronation velocity occurs.

Other selected parameters measured in rearfoot movement research include the following: (g) Achilles tendon angle—(Nigg) average angle formed between the midline of the heel and the medial horizontal during heel contact; (h) relative change of the Achilles tendon angle—(Nigg) within the first tenth of the foot contact period. This time interval was used because it corresponds to the duration of the passive forces in landing; (i) period of pronation—(Bates) the time of foot contact during which the foot is in a pronated position; and (j) takeoff angle—(Nigg, Bates) the angle between the lower leg and the calcaneus as the foot leaves the ground following the contact phase.

Several of the variables measured, such as maximum pronation

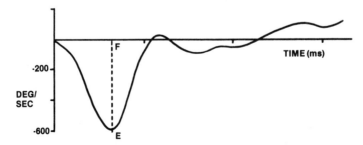

Figure 4 Angular velocity curve derived from the displacement data displayed in Figure 3. Parameters measured from these data are: E) maximum pronation velocity and F) time to maximum velocity.

and total rearfoot movement, would appear to be related to each other. Others are independent, as illustrated by our finding (Clarke et al., 1983b) that peak angular velocity was found to have no correlation with maximum pronation. At present, no evidence exists to indicate that there is any one rearfoot parameter that will predict the safety offered by a shoe or device.

Measurement Accuracy

When calculating angles, an error of ± 1 in 100 will produce an error on the order of 1 degree if one applies the error in a different direction for each line end point. Due to the relative closeness of heel angle markers, this angle is subject to significant errors if the image size is not sufficiently large to compliment the resolution of the digitizing setup so as to obtain the angle accuracy desired. For example, if the film image of the heel midline is 2 centimeters long, the resolution must be better than $\pm .2$ millimeters to insure that angle determination is better than ± 1 degree. Of course, one would hope for better accuracy than this. These calculations indicate the importance of maximizing the lower leg film image size.

Averaging Techniques

Each footfall that undergoes rearfoot film analysis is expensive to the researcher in terms of time spent digitizing and processing the data, and therefore it is important to know how much variability exists from step to step so that a minimum number of steps may be processed.

Bates et al. (1979) showed that for successive steps of the same foot, the time to maximum pronation varied by 12 milliseconds on average and maximum pronation varied by 0.3 degrees. As a result of this study, they stated "comparisons between the effects of two different shoes on the dynamic functioning of the leg would probably require the composite evaluation of several footfalls since the effects of shoes appear to be quite subtle."

In all their studies, Cavanagh et al. and Clarke et al. have averaged the results of three footfalls to produce composite scores for each foot analyzed. Two approaches to averaging such data will be presented here. The first approach is to average the three curves on a point-for-point basis beginning at foot strike, and then use an algorithm which determines the desired parameters from the average curve. The second approach is to use this same algorithm on the individual curves and to then arithmetically average these scores. One should remember that as long as the time sequence of rearfoot events remains the same, either technique is satisfactory. We compared these two techniques (Clarke et al., 1983b) on

360 subject/shoe combinations and found no difference in the results obtained by each technique.

Averaging results from different subjects in this fashion has the disadvantage that if anatomically similar events such as maximum pronation occur at different times, the resulting average curve shows an attenuated peak which does not reflect the average maximum observed. It would seem that average numerical data compiled from individual results is a more meaningful way to present group means than through the use of average curves.

Overground versus Treadmill Experimentation

As shown in Table 1, rearfoot movement experimentation has been conducted with subjects running overground on laboratory runways and on treadmills. The treadmill offers the advantage that the subject can run continuously at a controlled pace while several successive footfalls are filmed. The important question is whether treadmill running is a close enough facsimile of overground running to make results obtained on it generally applicable.

Dillman (1974) reviewed the biomechanical literature on overground versus treadmill running and reported that kinematic analyses have not yet shown any consistent differences between the two modes. We conducted a study to determine what differences exist in rearfoot parameters for the same subjects running under both conditions (Clarke et al., 1983b), and the results of this study are seen in Table 2. In this study, 10 subjects used a conventional running shoe while running at a 7-minute per mile pace on both a treadmill and a rubberized lab runway.

No significant differences were observed between the two testing situations. However, it should be noted that for all parameters measured, correlations of approximately .7 were obtained between both sets of individual results. The fact that these are only "fair" correlations indicates that some subjects may have been responding differently than others to the two different running sites. These results do prove that there exists no consistent altering of rearfoot parameters when experiments are conducted on a treadmill.

RESULTS OF REARFOOT STUDIES

As shown in Table 3, a review of several rearfoot studies revealed that a large number of subjects and conditions have been analyzed to determine rearfoot movement patterns during running. At the present time in the field of biomechanics, this many observations constitute a relatively large amount of experimentation. In this section an attempt will be made to summarize the key findings of this research.

TABLE 2 Mean Values—Rearfoot Movement Parameters for Treadmill versus Overground Running

	Touchdown Angle (Degrees)	Maximum Pronation (Degrees)	Time to Maximum Pronation (Milliseconds)	Maximum Pronation Velocity (Degrees per Second)	Time to Maximum Pronation Velocity (Milliseconds)
Treadmill	4.75	−11.28	89.5	−534	20.0
standard deviation	±4.76	±2.6	±16.4	±220	±5.0
Overground	5.13	−11.03	96.0	−510	27.5
standard deviation	±4.64	±1.8	±26.0	±202	±3.4

From Clarke et al. (1983b).

TABLE 3 Summary of Selected Results—Rearfoot Movement Studies Conducted by Various Researchers

Study	Condition	Pace (Meters per Second)	n	A	B	C	D	E	F	G	H	I	J
Bates (1978a)	Barefoot	3.8–4.5	10	1.9	−8.6	95	10.5					75.8	2.9
Bates (1978a)	Shoe	3.8–4.5	10	10.4	−7.2	82	17.6					53.9	12.3
Bates (1978a)	Shoe	3.3	10	8.8	−6.8	99	15.6					53.6	0.1
Bates (1979)	Shoe	4.5	11		−9.1	72						69.0	7.8
Bates (1980)	Shoe	4.1–4.9	2		−11.0	45							12.9
Cavanagh (1978)	Shoe	4.5	4				16.5	−789	15				
Cavanagh (1978)	Shoe/orthotic	4.5	4				10.0	−240	12				
Clarke (1980)	Shoe	4.5	15	3.7	−10.8	45	14.5						
Clarke (1983a)	Shoe	3.8	8	5.7	−11.4	94	17.1						
Clarke (1983a)	Shoe/orthotic	3.8	8	6.9	−8.9	102	15.8						
Clarke (1983b)	Shoe	3.8	10	4.9	−11.7	94	16.6	−532	27				
Nigg (1980)	Barefoot	3.0	54	0.8							3.9		2.9
Nigg (1980)	Shoes	3.0	45	7.5							6.3		12.3
Nigg (1981b)	Barefoot		47							−8.3			0.1
Nigg (1981b)	Shoes		47							−3.8			7.8
Nigg (1981b)	Shoes/orthotic		44							−0.1			12.9

Parameter key (see text for definitions)
A. Touchdown Angle (degrees)
B. Maximum Pronation Angle (degrees)
C. Time to Maximum Pronation (milliseconds)
D. Total Rearfoot Movement (degrees)
E. Maximum Pronation Velocity (degrees per second)
F. Time to Maximum Velocity (milliseconds)
G. Achilles Tendon Angle (degrees)
H. Achilles Tendon Movement (degrees)
I. Period of Pronation (percentage of contact)
J. Takeoff Angle (degrees)

Leg versus Heel Movement

From the definition of the rearfoot angle, it is clear that it is affected by changes in the position of either the leg or the heel during foot contact. All the research reviewed has indicated that the mean leg angle (from the vertical) has a value between 6 and 10 degrees of varus throughout foot contact, and for an individual varies by only 1 or 2 degrees throughout foot contact. Thus, changes in the rearfoot angle are largely caused by movement of the heel. However, the leg angle does affect the amount of pronation that is observed. Clarke et al. (1980) obtained the fair correlation of .73 between an increased leg angle at foot strike (varus) and maximum pronation observed. These data indicate a trend for more pronation in runners whose anatomy or whose running style causes them to plant their foot such that their leg angle is increased.

Effects of Speed Changes on Rearfoot Movement

The effects of increased speed upon rearfoot movement parameters have been measured directly by Bates et al. (1978a). They found no significant differences between running at 3.3 and 4.5 meters per second. Events such as maximum pronation occurred at the same percentage of total foot contact time. Other experiments have been conducted at a range of speeds (Table 3), and although results are not strictly comparable, no trends can be observed for commonly measured parameters.

Temporal Parameters

By using an accompanying side view camera, Bates et al. (1978b) have been able to describe rearfoot movement's temporal relationship to other kinematic events. They have shown that after being supinated at heel strike, a pronated posture of the subtalar joint occurs between 5 and 20% of foot contact. Maximum pronation and maximum knee flexion occurred at approximately the same time (35-40% of foot contact) and patella cross also occurred during this time period. The peroid of pronation in shoes was found to be 55 to 85% of total contact time.

Displacement and Velocity Parameters

If one examines the results in Table 3 and approximates the averages of all the results obtained from studies using various shoes, the model curve presented in Figure 5 would be generated. This curve was created by using the following input parameters: (a) total contact period = 220 milliseconds (estimated); (b) touchdown angle = 6.0 degrees (supination); (c) begin pronation = 10% of foot contact (22 milli-

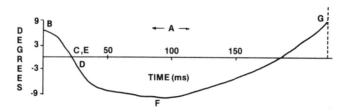

Figure 5 Model curve for rearfoot angular displacement generated from approximate averages of results from several rearfoot studies conducted by various researchers. Input parameters used were: A) total contact period = 220 ms, B) touchdown angle = 6.0°, C) begin pronation = 10% total contact time, D) maximum pronation velocity = 650° per second at 21 ms, E) total rearfoot movement in the first 10% of foot contact = 6.0°, F) maximum pronation = 9.4° at 90 ms, G) rearfoot angle at liftoff = 9.6°.

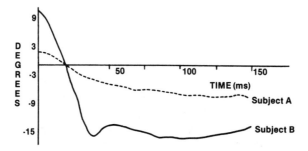

Figure 6 Range of variation in rearfoot angular displacement: mean rearfoot movement for two subjects. Note variation from model curve in Figure 5.

seconds); (d) maximum pronation velocity = 665 degrees per second at 21 milliseconds; (e) total rearfoot movement in the first 10% of foot contact = 6.0 degrees; (f) maximum pronation = 9.4 degrees at 90 milliseconds; and (g) rearfoot angle at lift-off = 9.6 degrees (supination).

This model curve provides a baseline summary from which other experimental results can be compared. It should be remembered that a wide range of individual values have been observed by various researchers. In Figure 6, data from two subjects (Clarke et al., 1983b) is shown to illustrate how individual subjects can vary from the average. In Table 4, the ranges of values are presented for a study involving 360 subject/shoe conditions. From these results, it is easy to see that the "typical" rearfoot angle curve must be viewed in the proper perspective.

Barefoot versus Shoes

Barefoot running is often looked upon as the baseline for normal running. The question that arises in testing barefoot runners is whether

TABLE 4   Mean Values—Midsole Flare, Cushioning, Heel Height Study

	Touchdown Angle (Degrees)	Maximum Pronation* (Degrees)	Time to Maximum Pronation (Milliseconds)	Total Rearfoot Movement* (Degrees)	Maximum Rearfoot Velocity (Degrees per Second)	Time to Maximum Velocity* (Milliseconds)
Mean	4.9	-11.7	93.6	16.6	-532	26.6
Standard deviation	3.9	3.6	22.6	3.7	173	8.2
Range	-4.2 to -15.4	-4.5 to -25.5	35.0 to 145.0	8.3 to 28.3	-206 to -1005	10.0 to 60.0

From Clarke et al. (1983b). (Each value obtained from 360 observations.)
*Significant differences (at an alpha level of .05) were observed between conditions for this variable.

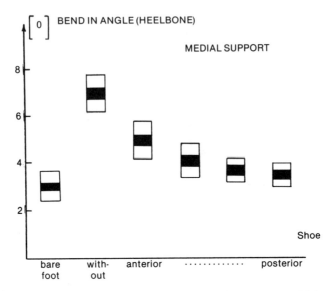

Figure 7 Data showing the amount of heel movement which occurred in the first 10% of foot contact for barefoot, shoe, and shoe
with orthotic conditions (Nigg et al., 1981a).

they are changing their style of running because of the lab or treadmill
experimental conditions. Bates et al. (1978a) and Nigg et al. (1980) have
shown a tendency for barefoot runners to strike the ground in a less
supinated position.

In Bates' study, removal of the shoe resulted in a statistically
significant increase in the period of pronation as a percentage of the support phase. Nigg et al. (1981a) have shown that the rearfoot angle at
takeoff is close to neutral (0 degrees) when running barefoot, and
significantly more supinated when shoes are used. They also showed that
running barefoot resulted in significantly less heelbone movement in the
first 10% of foot contact (Figure 7).

Use of Orthotics

As Harry Hlavac states in his book (1977), "Abnormal foot pronation should be corrected with orthotic devices." James (1978) conducted
a clinical study of the treatments of 232 running related injuries, and
reported that symptoms were relieved in 70% of the cases in which orthotics were prescribed. In various studies conducted to determine to
what extent orthotics alter rearfoot movement, orthotic devices have
been shown to significantly affect maximum pronation, total rearfoot
movement, time to maximum pronation, maximum pronation velocity,
the period of pronation, and the movement of the rearfoot angle in the
first 10% of foot contact.

Cavanagh et al. (1978) measured the effects of wearing orthotics of varying heights by having subjects run overground at a pace of 7 minutes per mile using one, two, and three layers of adhesive-backed felt, 6 millimeters thick, inserted along the medial border inside the subjects' shoes extending from the heel to approximately 55% of shoe length. They found approximately a 2-degree decrease in the amount of maximum pronation with each layer added. They also determined the rearfoot angular velocity by differentiating the displacement data, and the peak angular velocity also showed a progressive decrease as the thickness of the orthotic was increased. The results of this study for the control and 3-layer conditions are listed in Table 3.

Nigg et al. (1981a) have shown that systematically moving a medial support from an anterior to more posterior position reduces the change in heelbone angle, and therefore pronation, during the first 10% of foot contact (Figure 7). Clarke et al. (1983a) found significantly less maximum pronation when a 6-millimeter thick soft orthotic was inserted.

It is theorized that the mechanism with which soft orthotics cause a reduction in maximum pronation is two-fold. It provides a lift for the heel, which allows less ankle dorsiflexion throughout the contact phase with an accompanying reduction in pronation, since dorsiflexion is a component of pronation. In support of this point, Bates et al. (1978b) state that "the effect of a shoe with a slightly positive heel will reduce both the period and amount of pronation as well as the amount of maximum ankle dorsiflexion." They based this statement on the study of subjects running with and without a heel lift type of orthotic. Beyond the heel lift effect, it is felt that the orthotics support the arch, thus further limiting eversion of the calcaneus.

Based on the average inside geometry of running shoes, a 5mm medial lift causes a varus effect of approximately 5 degrees. The deformation of the shoe midsole and the orthotic itself probably accounts for the smaller 2- or 3-degree correction which accompanies each 5mm of lift.

Effects of Shoe Design

Cavanagh (1981) states in his book, "There is no doubt that the amount of pronation that occurs is dependent on the running shoe." The three components of Cavanagh's rearfoot control test (used in published consumer surveys) are the heel counter stiffness (stiffer is better), midsole penetration by an impact missle (less is better), and midsole deflection on impact at the lateral border of the outsole (less is better). In general, shoes with harder midsole materials, a stiffer counter, and wider heel base at the outsole will do relatively better on these tests.

Concerning the heel flare (explained in Figure 8), both Subotnick (1981) and Cavanagh (1981) have expressed the opinion that increased

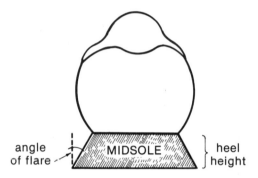

Figure 8 Rear view of a running shoe showing how heel flare and heel height are calculated.

medial flare is beneficial in that it can reduce pronation, while lateral flare is not beneficial because it can act as a lever arm that actually increases rearfoot angular velocity.

Cavanagh (1981) and Bates et al. (1980) have both shown that shoe design affects rearfoot parameters. To systematically test the effects of shoe design parameters, we tested three hardnesses of midsole materials, four heel heights, and three midsole flares in combination such that 36 specially made shoes were needed (Clarke et al., 1983b). The three midsole materials were all EVA foams: soft (25 durometer on a Shore A scale), medium (35 durometer) and hard (45 durometer). All three of these materials are found in running shoes currently being produced.

The measurement of heel height is illustrated in Figure 8, and the heights used were as follows: (a) 10mm midsole, no heel lift; (b) 10mm midsole with a 10mm heel lift; (c) 10mm midsole with a 20mm heel lift; (d) 20mm midsole with a 10mm heel lift. Heights 3 and 4 (the same overall heel height) allowed an examination of the effects of a heel lift upon rearfoot movement while removing the variable of overall heel height.

The heel flares were as follows: (a) 0 degrees, (b) 15 degrees, and (c) 30 degrees. They were obtained for each shoe from a knowledge of the heel height and width at the top and bottom of the midsole/wedge combination.

After the 36 shoes were constructed, they were closely inspected to insure that they closely matched the specifications previously described. Other features of the shoe were: (a) a curved last which was slip lasted in the fore part with an innersole board in the rear, and (b) a flat outsole, chosen to eliminate any possible effects of outsole pattern upon rearfoot movement.

As a frame of reference, at the present time the most commonly used midsole material is EVA foam with a durometer of 35. Midsole flares generally range from 2 to 25 degrees and heel heights from 20 to 30 millimeters, usually including a heel lift of 10 to 15 millimeters.

The conditions were presented to the subjects in random order and, after a 5-minute test period during which they ran for 2 minutes in each shoe, the film data was collected using a Photosonics Cine camera set at 200 frames per second. The subjects were allowed 2 or 3 minutes between each run to put on and secure the next shoe in sequence. An analysis of variance was used to determine the main and interactive effects of midsole hardness, heel height, and flare upon each rearfoot parameter. The Anova option of SPSS (Statistical Package for the Social Sciences) was used with an alpha level of .05 used to detect main and interactive significant differences.

The mean results, standard deviations, and ranges from the 360 subject/shoe conditions are shown in Table 4. As can be seen, wide ranges of values were demonstrated as the subjects responded to the different shoe conditions. Significant differences were observed for three of the variables: maximum pronation, total rearfoot movement, and the time to the maximum rearfoot velocity. None of the parameters measured displayed any interaction between the independent variables.

From the breakdown of significantly different category means, the following conclusions were made for comparisons of shoes that have similar design features:

1. Shoes having midsoles softer than 35 durometer will allow significantly more maximum pronation and total rearfoot movement.

2. Shoes having less rearfoot flare will allow more maximum pronation and total rearfoot movement.

3. Heel height has no significant effect on the amount or rate of pronation that occurs.

4. Time to maximum pronation velocity (actually inversely indicating the average angular acceleration) increases as the shoe becomes softer, has less flare and a lower heel lift.

These are important conclusions in that they provide the runner with the first experimentally based guidelines by which to select a shoe that will provide the best rearfoot control. These conclusions prove what has generally been arrived at empirically by coaches, clinicians, and runners themselves, and that is to wear a firmer shoe that is relatively wide at the outsole. The fact that there were no significant differences between the shoes having the same heel height but different amounts of heel lift contradicts some previous findings which stated that heel lift did affect rearfoot parameters (Bates et al., 1979).

Injuries and Rearfoot Movement

In his work on rearfoot movement in running, Nigg and his co-workers have attempted to link the occurrence of various leg ailments to particular patterns of rearfoot movement. In a study involving 84 subjects (1981b) running overground with 100cm stride lengths, they found that average pronation during heel contact was significantly greater in subjects with Achilles tendon pain, tendinitis at the tibia, and weaknesses in the ligaments than it was in those subjects who were experiencing no pain. In this same study, shoes with additional medial support inserted were found to reduce the average pronation of the subjects with symptoms to levels below those shown by symptom-free subjects in uncorrected shoes.

This type of research is probably the most important that can be done in this area in that it provides a way of identifying the movement parameters which indicate a predisposition to a certain type of injury. The effects of a shoe or orthotic device upon this parameter can then be measured to insure that the proper correction is being made.

Rearfoot Movement and Force Data

Due to the time involved for data reduction, an appealing alternative to filming runners in order to determine rearfoot movement would be to use information taken on-line from a force platform to predict this movement. One might theorize that either the center of pressure or medial-lateral force component would be related to rearfoot movement.

The most promising work to date along these lines has been by Nigg et al. (1981b), who showed that for subjects with no leg ailments versus those with pain, the center of pressure component in the direction of travel moved more uniformly (in time) from heel to toe. Since, as previously explained, the symptom-free subjects did exhibit less average pronation, this does seem to establish a relationship between force application and rearfoot movement. No direct correlation was made between these two parameters.

Cavanagh et al. (1978) directly examined the relationship between force and rearfoot parameters, as did Clarke et al. (1980). Of his study, Cavanagh stated, "The adaptations to the orthotics were clearly reflected in the changes seen in the center of pressure patterns. However the different patterns seen in the different subjects are an important statement about the individual nature of the response to an orthotic." It should be noted that these different patterns in center of pressure movement were accompanied by very consistent alterations in rearfoot movement. Clarke et al. (1980) were unable to establish anything more than weak correlations between rearfoot movement and the medial-lateral force and center of pressure components.

At the present time, it has not been proven that any force parameter can determine the magnitude of rearfoot movement or the changes in these movements caused by shoe design or the insertion of orthotics. By definition, the ground reaction forces will be affected by movements of all the body segments and therefore may be relatively insensitive to footwear changes. However, the advantages to be gained by being able to use this mode of experimentation as opposed to film demand that further study be made, particularly along the lines of Nigg's work.

SUMMARY AND RECOMMENDATIONS

The researcher embarking upon a study to measure some aspect of rearfoot movement has the advantage that a considerable number of similar studies have already been conducted, thus providing some guidelines for protocol and experimental direction. From the work reviewed in this paper, a number of methodological and directional recommendations can be made.

For conducting a rearfoot study, the following suggestions have been gleaned from the reviewed research: (a) Unless shoe design features are actually being measured, have all the subjects wear the same style of shoe because it has been proven that different shoes allow different amount of rearfoot movement. (b) Take care to insure that a line connecting the two leg markers is parallel to the long axis of the leg and that these marks can be placed consistently from day to day and subject to subject. This step is less important if results are to be reported in relative terms only (such as total rearfoot movements as opposed to maximum pronation). (c) Make sure that experimental shoes fit the subject well in the heel area so that monitoring the heel counter movement will be a valid means of predicting calcaneus movement. Also, consider a calibration scheme to account for slightly different orientations of the same shoes on the feet of different subjects.

Further suggestions are to: (d) Run the experiment either on a treadmill or overground, depending upon which is convenient, since no significant differences have been shown for rearfoot movement between the two modes. (e) Collect at least three footfalls of data for each subject/shoe condition since it has been shown that there is some step-by-step variablilty in rearfoot movement. (f) Since speed of running (within a 3.3-4.5 mps range) does not significantly affect rearfoot movement, conduct the experiment at a speed that can be comfortably handled by the subject group being tested.

When interpreting data obtained from the analysis of rearfoot film, consider the following: (a) Maximum pronation has been shown over a number of studies to average 9.4 degrees with a standard deviation within each study averaging approximately 3.5 degrees (where this could be obtained). Arbitrarily, it could be said that amounts of maximum pronation that are 13 degrees or greater are excessive in that they are outside one standard deviation for this parameter. (b) A similar argument for total rearfoot movement (which averaged 15.5 degrees) would indicate that ranges of 19.0 degrees or more are excessive. (c) In general, given the possibility for errors in placing heel and leg markers, more confidence can be placed in rearfoot parameters that measure relative, rather than absolute, rearfoot movement.

Three important areas for future study of rearfoot movement in running are the following: (a) relating clinical data to rearfoot movement parameters; (b) validating mechanical testing apparatus for rearfoot control in shoes; and (c) improving technology in order to allow on-line information to be obtained by clinicians.

In his work, Nigg has found that subjects who have leg ailments often display significantly different rearfoot characteristics. Future work along these lines would be to measure the effects of long-term adaptation to orthotics on rearfoot movement. Correlating foot type with rearfoot movement would be useful in shoe prescription, as would understanding how important it is to limit rearfoot movement in those runners who make first contact with the ground at a location further forward than their heels.

It is no secret that designing running footwear would be easier if mechanical testing apparatus could predict the amount of rearfoot control that a particular prototype would afford. Such apparatus would eliminate the need for expensive film studies for each shoe. The apparatus used by Cavanagh (1981) are founded upon theoretical bases which, in a general way, have been validated by our recent study (1983b). However, a specific validation must be made in which the kinematic parameters exhibited by subjects running in shoes are correlated with their relative rearfoot control ranking obtained by such apparatus.

Finally, it would be advantageous to clinicians if they could make rearfoot kinematic evaluations both before they prescribe corrective devices and after the subject is wearing them. However, the on-line film analysis equipment that presently exists is probably too expensive and temperamental to appear attractive to the clinician. Since rearfoot movement measurements involve tracking movement for four markers in one plane only, it may be possible to develop a dedicated tracking system using goniometric, laser, ultrasonic, video, or other techniques.

REFERENCES

Bates, B.T., Osternig, L.R., and Mason, B. Lower extremity function during the support phase of running. *Biomechanics VI*. Baltimore: University Park Press, **VI-B**:31-39, 1978a.

Bates, B.T., James, S.L., and Osternig, L.R. Foot function during the support phase of running. *Running* **3**(4):24-31, Fall 1978b.

Bates, B.T., Osternig, L.R., Mason, B.R., and James, S.L. Functional variability of the lower extremity during the support phase of running. *Medicine and Science in Sports* **11**:328-331, 1979.

Bates, B.T., Osternig, L.R., and Sawhill, J.A. *Effects of shoes on foot function.* Unpublished manuscript, 1980.

Cavanagh, P.R., Clarke, T.E., Williams, K.R., and Kalenak, A. *An evaluation of the effects of orthotics on pressure distribution and rearfoot movement during running.* Paper presented at the meeting of the American Orthopaedic Society for Sports Medicine, Lake Placid, NY, June 1978.

Cavanagh, P.R. *The running shoe book.* Mountain View, CA: World Publications, 1981.

Clarke, T.E., Lafortune, M.A., Williams, K.R., and Cavanagh, P.R. *The relationship between center of pressure location and rearfoot movement in distance running.* Paper presented at the meeting of the American College of Sports Medicine, Las Vegas, May 1980.

Clarke, T.E., Frederick, E.C., and Hlavac, H.F. The effects of a soft orthotic upon rearfoot movement in running. Accepted for publication in the *Journal of the American Academy of Podiatric Sports Medicine*, June 1983.

Clarke, T.E., Frederick, E.C., and Hamill, C. The effects of heel height, flare and midsole softness upon rearfoot control in running. Accepted for publication in *Medicine and Science in Sports and Exercise*, 1983.

Dillman, C.J. Kinematic analysis of running. *Exercise and Sports Sciences Reviews* **2**:193-218, 1974.

Hlavac, H.F. *The foot book.* Mountain View, CA: World Publications, 1977.

James, S.L., Bates, B.T., and Osternig, L.R. Injuries to runners. *Am. J. Sports Med.* **6**(2):40-50, 1978.

Jernick, S., and Heifitz, N.M. An investigation into the relationship of foot pronation to chondromalacia patellae. *Sports Medicine '79*, pp. 1-31, 1979.

Nigg, B.M., Eberle, G., Frey, D., Luethi, S., Segresser, B., and Weber, B. Gait analysis and sport-shoe construction. *Biomechanics VI* **VI-A**:303-309, 1978.

Nigg, B.M., Eberle, G., Frey, D., and Segresser, B. Biomechanische analyse von fubin suffizenzen. (Biomechanical analysis of the insufficient foot). *Medizinisch-Orthopadische Technik.*, pp. 178-180, June, 1977.

Nigg, B.M., and Luethi, S. Bewegungsanalysen bein laufschuh. (Movement analysis and running shoes). *Sport Wissenschaft.* **3**:309-320, 1980.

Nigg, B.M., Denoth, J., Luethi, S., and Stacoff, A. *Methodological aspects of sport shoe and sport floor analysis.* Paper presented to the International Congress of Biomechanics, Nagoya, Japan, July 1981a.

Nigg, B.M., Luethi, S., Stacoff, A., and Segresser, B. *Biomechanical effects of pain and sport shoe connections.* Paper given during an Australian Sports Biomechanics lecture tour, August 1981b.

Schuster, R.O. Biomechanical running problems. Sports Medicine '78, pp. 43-54, 1978.

Subtonick, S.I. The flat foot. *Physician & Sports Med.* **9**(8):85-91, August 1981.

CHAPTER ELEVEN

The Effect of Running Shoe Design on Shock Attenuation

E.C. Frederick, T.E. Clarke, and C.L. Hamill

There are many unanswered questions about what constitutes good cushioning in a sport shoe. We can't help matters much with definitions. For example, if we define *cushioning* as the attenuation of peak forces, and further define *good cushioning* as the attenuation of those forces to levels that can be tolerated by the musculoskeletal system, we have only raised more questions that cannot be answered.

What forces must cushioning systems attenuate? Surely not all forces are to be lessened. After all, some, such as propulsive forces, are important to performance. What are the tolerable magnitudes of those forces? This is a complex issue that involves, among other things, a knowledge of the response of various musculoskeletal structures to repeated stress and detailed information on the magnitude of the forces in question. Little of this type of information exists.

On the surface it seems as though we have made no progress in our research on cushioning. While it is true that we have few answers, we have advanced our definition of the problem considerably in the last decade.

Using force platforms, Cavanagh and Lafortune (1980), Frederick et al., (1981), and Nigg et al., (1982, 1983) have determined that during running the magnitude of vertical force between the ground and the foot is of the order of two to three times the runner's weight. Two force peaks typically occur: an impact peak rising in the first 20 to 30 msec after footstrike, and a propulsive or active peak occurring roughly 100 msec after footstrike.

When one recalls that both feet strike the ground some 1,500 times per mile, it seems reasonable that repeated loadings of a magnitude of two to three times body weight might produce negative biological effects if they are not attenuated. Radin et al. (1982) and Voloshin and Wosk (1982) have shown, for example, that a lack of sufficient shock attenuation is linked to degenerative changes in joints and to low back pain. It is presumed that many of the chronic musculoskeletal disorders that athletes present are at least exacerbated by repeated impact loadings (Bates et al., 1982; Nigg et al., 1982, 1983). This brings us to the issue of quantifying the shock attenuating properties of sport shoes and, in particular, running shoes.

Although confusing results have been reported from studies comparing material tests of running shoes with measurements of vertical ground reaction forces, while wearing the same shoes (Bates et al., 1982; Nigg et al., 1983; Clarke et al., 1983a), the material tests are still necessary as a reference point—an indicator of the *in vitro* shock attenuating properties of various shoe designs.

Clarke et al. (1983b) have suggested that the unexpected lack of correlation between the material test results performed on the shoes alone and the actual force platform data collected with subjects running in the shoes is perhaps due to the fact that the body is adjusting its kinematics in response to the perceived hardness of the shoe. This adaptation changes the ground reaction force pattern that is recorded and so hides any shock absorbing effect that might be produced by the physical properties of the shoe. The observation that runners respond to the physical characteristics of the shoe underlines the importance of accurately measuring those physical characteristics.

About 80% of runners land heel first and exhibit the typical two-peaked vertical ground reaction force curve (Cavanagh & LaFortune, 1980; Kerr et al., 1983). These two peaks in force are localized in different regions of the shoe (Cavanagh, 1978). The impact peak occurs when the center of pressure is in the center of the heel of the shoe, and the active peak when the center of pressure is located under the ball of the foot.

These observations provided a rationale for the development of an impact tester by Cavanagh and his co-workers at Penn State University (Cavanagh, 1978, 1980; Cavanagh et al., 1980). This device drops a weighted shaft a distance of 5 cm onto the surface of the heel or forefoot of the sockliner in the shoes. The shaft is instrumented to provide a record of either acceleration or force (which in turn is converted to acceleration).

The output from this impact tester is a value for peak deceleration of the missile or "peak g." Lower peak g scores are consistent with better shock attenuation. Typical peak g values range from 9g to 12g for the heel of a running shoe and from 11g to 15g for the forefoot (Cavanagh, 1980).

METHODS AND MATERIALS

Impact Tester

The device used in this study to analyze impact shock attenuating properties of various shoe designs consists of a cylindrical 7.3 kg metal shaft which slides freely in the vertical plane. The head of the shaft is a round, flat-bottomed metal disc of radius 1.25 cm to which is attached a Kistler piezoelectric force transducer. A check of the velocity of the shaft at impact was made with an ultrasonic velocity transducer. Output from both transducers was collected online with a DEC PDP 11/34 mini-computer.

The shaft was dropped from a height of 5 cm onto the heel or forefoot region of the shoe. The sockliner was left in place to produce a more realistic estimate of the cushioning properties of the shoes as they are used. Five impacts were made on each test shoe before a value was taken.

Experimental Shoes

To systematically test the effects of shoe design parameters, we tested three hardnesses of midsole materials, four heel heights, and three angles of midsole flare. In total, 36 specially made shoes were analyzed. The three midsole materials were all Ethylene Vinyl Acetate (EVA) foams in one of three hardnesses: soft (25 durometer on Shore A scale), medium (35 durometer) and hard (45 durometer). All three of these foams can be found in running shoes currently being produced.

The range of sole geometries as defined by the heel heights and angles of midsole flare used in the test shoes are shown in Figure 1. The heights used were as follows: 10mm midsole + zero heel wedge; 10mm midsole + 10mm wedge; 10mm midsole + 20mm wedge; and 20mm midsole + 10mm wedge. The last two combinations have the same overall heel height but differ in the heel lift produced by the wedge. These two configurations were used to test the relative effects of heel lift versus heel height on rearfoot control (see Chapter 8). They would be expected to have little if any effect on cushioning in the heel area so their results are treated as a single variable in the heel impact tests.

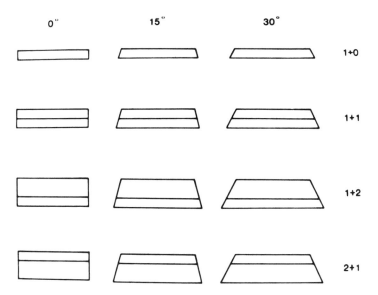

Figure 1   Sole geometry in cross-section of shoes used in study. All combinations shown also made up in three hardnesses. Thickness of midsole plus wedge is indicated in centimeters in right-hand column. Angle of flare shown above in degrees.

Forefoot cushioning, however, should obviously be affected by the thicker forefoot of the 20mm + 10mm configuration, and so those data were collected and are reported. A range of sole thickness of from 10mm to 30mm covers the extremes that can be found in mass produced running shoes.

The angles of heel flare found on the experimental shoes were: 0 degrees, 15 degrees, and 30 degrees. The actual angles were calculated from the arctangent of half the difference between the width of the top and bottom of the wedge/midsole divided by the total height of this combination. A range of flares of from 0 to 25 degrees represents the range of actual angles found in running shoes produced in recent years. In the past, shoes with 30-degree angles of flare have been produced.

After the 35 shoes were constructed, they were closely inspected to insure that they matched specifications. All shoes were constructed on a curved last which was slip lasted in the forepart and with an innersole board in the rear. The shoes were also constructed with the same flat outsole to control for any effects that outsole design might have on impact characteristics.

As a frame of reference for readers who are not familiar with shoe construction techniques, most running shoes used primarily for training are constructed on a curved last with a full-length innersole board. They also use approximately 35 durometer EVA foam and have the 10mm +

10 mm (or a 10mm + 15mm) heel lift configuration and roughly 15 degrees of midsole flare.

RESULTS

Table 1 displays the results of impact tests on the heel of all 27 shoes used in the study (heel height 10mm + 20mm was not included). A glance at the data reveals that heel height and hardness had a greater influence on the impact scores than the angle of flare. In fact, a three-way analysis of variance on hardness (durometer), flare, and heel height against peak g reveals nonsignificant effects due to flare (see Table 2).

If we ignore the angle of flare as a variable we can graph, in a 3-D plot, the effects of both heel thickness and hardness on peak g. Figure 2 is such a plot and it shows the nonlinear effect of hardness on peak g. Going from 25 to 35 durometer hardness in the 10mm + 10mm thickness raises peak g by 27%, but going from 35 to 45 durometers raises peak g by 38%. The effect of thickness is similarly nonlinear in the soft durometer (25 Shore A). But, as might be expected, this effect disappears in the harder shoes perhaps because of the greater surface elastic behavior of these shoes.

By "surface elastic" we mean that in harder materials impact forces tend to be distributed over a larger area because of the stiffness of the structure. Softer materials, on the other hand, behave in a more "point elastic" manner with the impact affecting mostly the material just under the point of impact.

The results of the forefoot impact tests were similar to the heel impact score when similar thicknesses and hardnesses are compared. The

TABLE 1   Impact Score (Peak g) for Rearpart of Shoes with Various Combinations of Flare, Heel Height, and Hardness

Hardness (Shore A Durometer)	Flare (°)	Heel Height (mm) 10	20	30
25	0	14.5	10.5	9.8
	15	14.4	10.8	10.1
	30	14.6	11.1	10.3
35	0	15.8	13.3	11.2
	15	16.9	13.3	12.7
	30	16.0	14.8	12.7
45	0	20.4	18.4	14.2
	15	19.4	17.1	13.6
	30	19.2	18.6	14.9

TABLE 2   Three-way Analysis of Variance of Shoe Hardness (Durometer), Flare, and Heel Height

Source of Variation		Anova Table df	ss	ms	F.
A	Hardness	2	133.950	66.980	11.173*
B	Heel height	2	85.150	42.580	35.362*
C	Flare	2	1.250	0.625	0.183
A × B		4	13.690	3.422	0.967
A × C		4	24.450	6.112	1.728
B × C		4	3.350	0.837	0.237
A × B × C		8	764.070	3.537	

Dependent variable is rearfoot impact score.
*Significant F.05 (2,8) = 4.46; F.05 (4,8) = 3.84

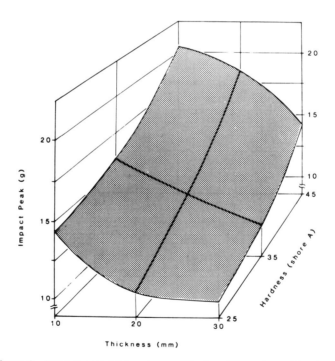

Thickness (mm)

Figure 2   Impact peak (g) for shoes with nine different combinations of hardness and sole thickness. Sole thickness is shown on the x-axis, hardness on the y-axis and peak g on the z-axis. Each of the nine data points represents a shoe with a particular combination of hardness and thickness.

TABLE 3   Forefoot Impact (g) for Two Thicknesses
and Three Different Hardnesses of Material

	Hardness (Shore A Durometer)		
Thickness (mm)	25	35	45
10	11.9	13.2	16.5
20	9.6	10.3	15.3

slightly lower scores are probably due to the fact that the shoes were slip lasted in the forefoot—a process that leaves only the upper fabric between the sockliner and the top of the midsole. This type of construction eliminates the board found in the rearpart which distributes the impact load over a broader area, thus making the compressive stiffness of board-lasted shoes higher.

DISCUSSION

These results indicate that sole thickness and hardness (as measured by the traditional Shore A durometer) are related to peak g in a nonlinear fashion, that is, increasing sole thickness from 10 to 20mm has much more effect than from 20 to 30mm, and decreasing durometer from 45 to 35 has more of an effect than from 35 to 25. This is an important factor to keep in mind when choosing or designing a running shoe. Effects that would seem to produce arithmetic changes in cushioning can actually increase or decrease the peak g exponentially.

Questions frequently arise about the appropriateness of the shaft weight and drop height used in impact tests. Cavanagh, Valiant, and Misevich (1983) and Misevich and Cavanagh (1983) have discussed how the response of the shoe to impact is affected by missile head velocity and missile weight. Their observations and the fact that we are trying to simulate the impact of the foot and shoe with the ground underline the importance of using an appropriate input energy for the missile.

In general, the parameters we have selected (Cavanagh, 1980) are considered appropriate for simulating heel impact even though the time to peak acceleration that we observe is short (6-8 msec), relative to the time to peak of the first peak of the vertical ground reaction force curve ($\sim$20-30 msec), and the pressures generated ($\sim$700 kPa) are not high enough to simulate the peak pressures of 1.5 mPa measured by Cavanagh and Hennig (1983) in running. Even though their peak pressure data were much higher than the pressures generated by our impact tester, it should be pointed out that the peak pressures reported by

Cavanagh and Hennig were localized in a 1 cm^2 area whereas our impact tester values are distributed by the missile head over an area of 4.9 cm^2. This tends to reduce the peak pressure values, but it may represent a more realistic summary of the impact of the whole heel area of the foot when peak impact is reached.

Recommendations

These data on the effect of various design features on the cushioning characteristics of running shoes should prove useful to people interested in designing sport shoes or in selecting from the variety of products currently on the market. When these data are combined with the data presented by Clarke et al. in Chapter 10 on the effects of design parameters on rearfoot control, a few recommendations can be made.

When choosing a shoe with more cushioning, picking a thicker soled shoe is a wiser choice than a softer shoe. Thicker soles have no effect on maximum pronation, but increased thickness can increase cushioning significantly. Choosing a softer rather than thicker sole, however, would mean significantly less rearfoot control. The optimal combination of rearfoot control and cushioning occurs in thickly soled shoes with a 35 durometer midsole/wedge, flared to 15 degrees.

Not surprisingly, this is close to the characteristics of the average shoe generally worn for training today, although there has been a disturbing tendency in recent years toward the development of softer rather than thicker soled designs. These softer soled designs may be fine for many runners, but they also may have negative consequences for those runners who need good rearfoot control in their training shoes.

Similar recommendations should hold for racing shoes where low weight without a loss of cushioning is the objective. It may be possible, however, to fine tune the design of racing flats even further with slightly thinner and slightly softer soles which would lighten the shoes while maintaining cushioning, yet minimally compromising rearfoot control. These data indicate only that such an approach may be fruitful to shoe designers, but an empirical approach is still needed.

REFERENCES

Bates, B.J., James, S.L., Osternig, L.P., Sawhill, J.A., and Hamill, J. Effects of running shoes on ground reaction forces. In: A. Morecki and K. Fidelus (eds.), *Biomechanics VII*. University Park Press, Baltimore, 1982.

Cavanagh, P.R. A technique for averaging center of pressure paths from a force platform. *J. Biomech.* **11**:487-491, 1978.

Cavanagh, P.R. Testing procedure. *Runner's World*, pp. 70-80, Oct. 1978.

Cavanagh, P.R. *The running shoe book*. Anderson World, Mountain View, CA, 1980.

Cavanagh, P.R., and Hennig, E.M. Pressure distribution measurement — A review and some new observations on the effect of shoe foam materials during running. In: B.M. Nigg and B.A. Kerr (eds.), *Biomechanical aspects of sport shoes and playing surfaces*, pp. 187-190. University of Calgary, Canada, 1983.

Cavanagh, P.R., Hinrich, R.N., and Williams, K.R. Testing procedure for the runner's world shoe survey. *Runner's World*, pp. 38-49, Oct. 1980.

Cavanagh, P.R., and LaFortune, M.A. Ground reaction forces in distance running. *J. Biomech.* **13**:397-406, 1980.

Cavanagh, P.R., Valiant, G.A., and Misevich, K.W. Biological aspects of modelling shoe/foot interaction during running. In: E.C. Frederick (ed.), *Sport shoes and playing surfaces*. Human Kinetics, Champaign, IL, 1983.

Clarke, T.E., Frederick, E.C., and Cooper, L.P. Effects of shoe cushioning upon ground reaction forces in running. *Int. J. Sports Med.* **4**, 1983. (a)

Clarke, T.E., Frederick, E.C., and Cooper, L.P. Biomechanical measurement of running shoe cushioning properties. In: B.M. Nigg and B.A. Kerr (eds.), *Biomechanical aspects of sport shoes and playing surfaces*, pp. 25-33. University of Calgary, Canada, 1983. (b)

Frederick, E.C., Hagy, J.L., and Mann, R.A. The prediction of vertical impact force during running. *J. Biomech.* **14**:498, 1981.

Kerr, B.A., Beauchamp, L., Fisher, V., and Neil, R. Footstrike patterns in distance running. In: B.M. Nigg and B.A. Kerr (eds.), *Biomechanical aspects of sport shoes and playing surfaces*, pp. 135-142. University of Calgary, Canada, 1983.

Misevich, K.W., and Cavanagh, P.R. Material aspects of modelling shoe/foot interaction. In: E.C. Frederick (ed.), *Sport shoes and playing surfaces*. Human Kinetics, Champaign, IL, 1984.

Nigg, B.M., Denoth, J., Kerr, B., Luethi, S., Smith, D., and Stacoff, A. Load, sport shoes and playing surfaces. In: E.C. Frederick (ed.), *Sport shoes and playing surfaces*. Human Kinetics, Champaign, IL, 1984.

Nigg, B.M., Denoth, J., Luethi, S., and Stacoff, A. Methodological aspects of sport shoe and sport floor analysis. In: H. Matsui and K. Kobayashi (eds.), *Biomechanics VIII-B*, pp. 1041-1052. Human Kinetics, Champaign, IL, 1983.

Nigg, B.M., Denoth, J., and Neukomm, P.A. Quantifying the load on the human body. In: A. Morecki and K. Fidelus (eds.), *Biomechanics VII*, pp. 88-105. University Park Press, Baltimore, 1982.

Radin, E.L., Orr, R.B., Kelman, J.L., Paul, I.L., and Rose, R.M. Effects of prolonged walking on concrete on the knees of sheep. *J. Biomech.* **15**:487-492, 1982.

Voloshin, A., and Wosk, J. An in vivo study of low back pains and shock absorption in the human locomotor system. *J. Biomech.* **15**:21-27, 1982.